...He Will Give You
ANOTHER
HELPER

...He Will Give You ANOTHER HELPER

A Complete Understanding of the Holy Spirit's Role in Our Lives

by

Marilyn Hickey

Harrison House
Tulsa, Oklahoma

...He Will Give You Another Helper—
A Complete Understanding of the Holy Spirit's Role in Our Lives
ISBN 1-57794-378-3
Copyright © 2001 by Marilyn Hickey
P.O. Box 17340
Denver, Colorado 80217

05 04 03 02 01   5 4 3 2 1

Published by Harrison House, Inc.
P. O. Box 35035
Tulsa, Oklahoma 74135

Contents

Introduction

God has a wonderful destiny for your life, and He has given the Holy Spirit as your Helper to guarantee your success. Your part is to ask for His help, receive it, and become obedient to His direction.

I desire for this book to help you explore the personality of the Holy Spirit in all His facets. I want to teach you about His calling, gifts, and function in us. Discover His role in the Old Testament, and contrast that with the New Testament lives of Spirit-filled saints.

We will examine the book of Acts and experience the Holy Spirit, interacting with believers, working in and through them for ministry. I believe God is pouring out His Spirit today. He told us not to be drunk with wine, wherein is excess; but the early Church certainly drank of the "new wine" of the Holy Spirit. Yet, I remember that He saves His best wine till last! I believe that these are the days of the best wine. I wholeheartedly encourage you to drink deeply of this "new wine."

The presence of His Holy Spirit is flowing and available through this book. I also believe He will flow through the personal experiences you will have in the days to come, especially after you have looked closely at the work of the Spirit in times past. I encourage you to spend time in His presence and allow Him to reveal Himself to you. Learn why it is so vitally important to know God's manifest presence through the Holy Spirit in your life today.

Whether you've just been introduced to the things of God, or you've long drunk of the Spirit, I pray that you will find the Holy Spirit to be Another Helper and learn of Him in a deeper, more intimate way.

Chapter 1

You Can Know the One Jesus Promised

To live and function as God wills, we as believers need the Holy Spirit's anointing working in us and through us. Jesus promised Him to every believer; all we have to do is ask:

> **"If you then, being, know how to give good gifts to your children, how much more will your heavenly Father give the Holy Spirit to those who ask him!"**
>
> **Luke 11:13**

The Holy Spirit wants the Body of Christ to know Him and desires to become very real to us. Sometimes we refer to the Holy Spirit as *It*, or as *the Anointing*. The person of the Holy Spirit is not an *it.* Jesus never referred to Him that way. The Holy Spirit is also not simply your prayer language. We must realize that praying in tongues according to Acts 2:4 is not the full gift of the Holy Spirit. The Holy Spirit is a person, and He desires a relationship with us on a daily basis.

Let's look at the words of Jesus right before He went to the cross in John 14-16. He taught more on the Holy Spirit at the Last Supper than at any other time, and He said the most important things to His disciples right before He went to the cross.

Today you do the same thing when you tell your children the things you want them to remember just before you leave the house You say, "Now, be good, go to bed on time, and mind the babysitter."

Jesus tells them that He's going to leave but that He wouldn't leave them comfortless. He would send the Holy Spirit to comfort them. (John 14:16,18.)

The Holy Spirit talks to you.

In chapters 14 through 16, Jesus used the pronouns *He, Him,* and *Himself* nineteen times when describing the Holy Spirit, and by this, Jesus indicates that the third part of the Trinity is a personality.

When you think of Him that way, it's easier to see the traits of His personality. For example, one way you know a person is a person and not an it is because a person *talks* to you. The Holy Spirit talks to you.

He can drop a little chorus in our hearts or give us a Scripture or a vision. He fellowships with us individually so that we don't have to just know *about* the Holy Spirit; we can experience Him intimately, personally, each day.

The Holy Spirit was assigned to you as a helper long before you knew Him. The Bible tells us that the Holy Spirit knew you in the womb. He knew you and had a plan for your life. (Jer. 1:5.) He was intimately involved with you in your conception and in your forming. He sees you as unique to the plan of God.

The Holy Spirit in the Life of Jesus

The Holy Spirit is the presence of God. He is the invisible presence of the Spirit who makes the heavenly Father and His Son, Jesus Christ, known in the earth. The person of the Spirit is ever present in the affairs of humanity, breathing life into all God's plans.

Throughout the ages, the Spirit has cast His shadow over the earth, from creation (Gen. 1:1) to this very day. It was the life-giving presence of the Holy Spirit who came to the Virgin Mary, and by His power she conceived Jesus, who was the visible presence of God:

> **He sees you as unique to the plan of God.**

> **"The Holy Spirit will come upon you, and the power of the Most High will overshadow you. So the holy one to be born will be called the Son of God"**
>
> **Luke 1:35** NIV

The Holy Spirit is the person of the Trinity who is present in the earth today. Without drawing attention to Himself, the Spirit acquaints us with the Father and the Son. The divine presence of the Holy Spirit bridges the distance between heaven and earth, revealing God's thoughts to us and communicating our thoughts to God.

When Mary visited Elizabeth, the Holy Spirit filled both their mouths with praise and prophecy. The Spirit was the inspiration of their worship, and He authored the prophetic revelation of the Savior, whom Mary carried in her womb:

> **. . . Elizabeth was filled with the Holy Spirit. In a loud voice she exclaimed: "Blessed are you among women, and blessed is the child you will bear! But why am I so favored, that the mother of my Lord should come to me?" And Mary said: 'My soul glorifies the Lord and my spirit rejoices in God my Savior'**
>
>

Luke 1:41-43,46,47 NIV

The Holy Spirit led both Simeon and Anna into the temple and, through prophecy, revealed the baby in Mary's arms as our Redeemer. (Luke 2:25-32.) Filling human vessels with God's revelation, the Spirit spoke God's will of carrying out His grand design of salvation and redemption into the earth.

> **Lord, now lettest thou thy servant depart in peace, according to thy word: for mine eyes have seen thy salvation.**
>
>

Luke 2:29,30

Simeon knew that Jesus was the Messiah because the Holy Spirit revealed it to him.

The Holy Spirit sets divine power in motion through the anointing. Upon those who receive His anointing, His presence comes with dynamic authority, ability, and power. From the moment the Holy Spirit came upon Jesus at His baptism in the Jordan, He was anointed with power that had no limitation:

> **. . . Jesus was baptized... and the Holy Spirit descended on him in bodily form like a dove . . .**
>
>

Luke 3:21,22

For the one [Jesus] whom God has sent speaks the words of God, for God gives the Spirit without limit

John 3:34 NIV

When John the Baptist baptized Jesus, the Bible says the Spirit came down upon Him, and Jesus was baptized in the Holy Spirit. Suddenly John recognized Jesus as the Son of God and said, "I don't need to baptize You; You need to baptize me, because You're going to baptize me with the Holy Ghost and fire." (Matt. 3:11-17.)

Apparently John was an opportunist, knew the baptism of the Holy Spirit was coming, and wanted to get in on it early! He already had the Spirit upon him, leading him, but he didn't know the fullness of the Spirit.

John wasn't a part of the dispensation to be baptized with the Holy Spirit and with fire, which came at the Day of Pentecost, *but he saw it.* The Holy Spirit leads us into truth and shows us things to come. (John 16:13.) *Jesus left Jordan to face the devil, but what the devil didn't know is that he'd have to face the Holy Spirit.* The Holy Spirit led Jesus into the wilderness, where Satan tempted him. (Luke 4:1-13.)

> **The Holy Spirit leads us into truth and shows us things to come.**

That always shocks me when I read that. Why would the Holy Spirit lead Jesus into a place where Satan would besiege Him with temptations? Hebrews 4:15 tells us that Jesus was tempted in all ways as we are and overcame them in order to be our Savior and example. Therefore, the Holy Spirit indeed led Jesus into the wilderness not only to be tempted, but also to triumph over the temptation.

13

The Bible also tells us that Jesus came out of the wilderness in the power of the Holy Spirit. (Luke 4:14.) The anointing was upon Him, Jesus was full of power, and He overcame Satan's temptation. Afterward, Jesus returned to Galilee in that same Holy Spirit power, and He began a ministry marked by profound preaching and teaching, punctuated by miracles of deliverance and healing:

Jesus, full of the Holy Spirit, returned from the Jordan and was led by the Spirit in the desert.

Jesus returned to Galilee in the power of the Spirit, and news about him spread through the whole countryside.

Luke 4:1,14 NIV

> **Like Jesus, we can successfully overcome trials and temptations in the power of the Holy Spirit.**

Like Jesus, we can successfully overcome trials and temptations in the power of the Holy Spirit.

Everything Jesus did, He did by the power of the Holy Spirit. In fact, Jesus did not cleanse a leper, heal the sick, open blind eyes, or perform any other miracles *until He was baptized in the Holy Spirit.*

Jesus said, "I don't do anything unless the Father shows Me. I only do what the Father shows Me." (John 14:10.) But He could not do any of those things that the Father showed Him without the help of the Holy Spirit. John 14:6 says. "If you've seen me you've seen the Father"—because they are 1 God in 3 persons—yet still all God.

When Jesus prayed in the Garden of Gethsamene before His crucifixion, the Holy Spirit ministered to Him. When He died on the cross, He laid down His life through the power of the Holy Spirit and was raised from the dead by the power of the Holy Spirit!

The Holy Spirit is a person who dwells and communicates with us. He desires to help us by becoming intimately involved in every area of our lives.

The Gift of the Holy Spirit

Jesus gave the very best gift He could give you to help you succeed in this life—the Holy Spirit. He is God's gift to us. Remember, Jesus said, "I'm going to ask the Father to give you another Comforter, the Holy Spirit." (John 14:16.)

The word *ask* is a very strong word. It is a legal word. Jesus is saying, "I have a legal right to ask the Father to give you the Holy Spirit." He didn't say that the gift would be given according to how good you are or how sweet your disposition is—or for that matter, according to how bad you are or how unpleasant your disposition is. The Holy Spirit is a *gift,* and He will make you good enough! He gives life to you, empowers you, and takes you through temptation.

> **Jesus gave the very best gift He could give you to help you succeed in this life—the Holy Spirit.**

When Jesus said He would send us the Holy Spirit, He said He would give us *"another* Comforter." Jesus is a Comforter. John 14:10. If you were walking with Jesus in the flesh, wouldn't it be a tremendous comfort? If you had a problem, you could say, "Jesus, could You tell me what to do about this?" or, "Jesus, I have a pain in my side. Would You just put Your hand right there?" Imagine what a comfort He would be!

I looked up the modern word *comfort.* It's Latin and divides into two parts—*com* and *fortis,* meaning "with strength."[1]

If we will follow the Holy Spirit's leading by seeking to live a balanced, healthy lifestyle that includes appropriate amounts of work, exercise, ministry, rest and play, He will keep us full of strength.

Sometimes I hear people say, "I'm just so tired—I'm burned out." I don't believe that people who stay full of the Holy Spirit need to experience burnout. If we will follow the Holy Spirit's leading by seeking to live a balanced, healthy lifestyle that includes appropriate amounts of work, exercise, ministry, rest, and play, He will keep us full of strength.

According to Jesus, the Holy Spirit is another Comforter—Jesus being the first. There are two different connotations for the word *another*. It can mean another thing of the same kind or another of a different kind.

So Jesus wasn't sending us a different kind of Comforter; He was saying, "I'm going to send you *the same kind* of Comforter I've had all this time. He was with Me when I was building the earth, and all the time I was on the earth. The same kind of Comforter who brought Me through will also bring you through."

What a blessing! Jesus gave us the gift of the Holy Spirit—the same Comforter who comforted *Him*.

The Holy Spirit's Calling

The word *comforter* in the Greek is probably more meaningful to you and me of what Jesus is saying there. It's *paracletos*—paraclete.[2]

Para means "to come alongside."[3] The Greek word *kalayo* is what *kletos* comes from and means "to call."[4] The Holy Spirit is *called* to come alongside you, stay with you, and take you through troubles.

I hear people saying all the time, "I'm called to street evangelism," or, "I'm called to teach Sunday school," or, "I'm called to intercede for others." Did it ever occur to you that the Holy Spirit also has a calling? He's called to come alongside and hold on to you, to bring you through the trials and temptations of life.

Remember, the Holy Spirit is a person, and He's called to *be with you* as long as you live. John 14:16 promises He will abide with you forever.

He Is a Person: Characteristics of the Holy Spirit

Every person has personality traits. The person of the Holy Spirit is no different.

One aspect of His personality is that there is joy in His presence. Did you know that you can get *ecstatic* in the presence of the Lord? I mean, you can experience joy like nothing else. If you've ever had the joy of the Holy Spirit hit you, you know that it's the most refreshing thing in the world, and it's scriptural. The Bible talks about the joy the Holy Spirit gives: "In thy presence is fullness of joy" (Ps. 16:11).

The Holy Spirit is a personality; therefore, you can grieve Him. He is grieved when you don't listen to Him. He's the Spirit of Truth; therefore, He is always trying to lead you in the right direction. When you want to go your own way and tell Him to "bug off," you frustrate His call.

How many times have you walked into trouble and the Holy Spirit tried to stop you, but you didn't take heed? Then you thought, "I'll bet God is mad at me." Neither God nor Jesus are mad at you, but They are concerned. The Holy Spirit, on the other hand, is weeping over you when you miss or ignore His leading.

In John 3, God gives a beautiful picture of the Holy Spirit. This is the story of Nicodemus, the man who came to Jesus by night to ask how to be born again. During the course of His explanation, Jesus compared the Holy Spirit to a wind: "The wind blows wherever it pleases . . . " (John 3:8). You can feel the wind, but you can't see it. Likewise, you can feel the Holy Spirit, but you can't see Him.

When the Holy Spirit comes into your heart and bears witness that you belong to Jesus, like the wind, He bends and directs you out of the flesh and puts you into the supernatural. When you tell people that you are born again, they may not understand what the term means; but when they see your life blown, bent, and directed by the "wind" of the Holy Spirit, they will know there is something different about you.

Ezekiel 37:9,10 says that the "breath" of the spirit came upon those who were dead and brought them to life! When the Holy Spirit breathed on you at your new birth, He gave you life. Sometimes He comes like a gale, and sometimes He's like a gentle breeze. Jesus breathed the new birth into His disciples: "he breathed on them and said, 'Receive the Holy Spirit'" (John 20:22).

The Holy Spirit: Acceptable and Accessible Through Jesus

Jesus told us what the Holy Spirit did through Him by enabling and empowering Him—but He also taught about Him, thus making the Holy Spirit an acceptable part of the believer's experience.

For the Spirit to remain and abide on the earth, He, like Jesus, needed a birthplace. Prior to Pentecost, the Holy Spirit had never remained on anyone but Jesus. On the day of Pentecost, however, the Holy Spirit came to earth and was birthed in the human race. No longer would He "come" and "go." He would now "abide" with men.

When you were born again, the Holy Spirit was born in you. Jesus promised in John 14:16 that He would send the Holy Spirit to ". . . be with you forever." Whether you are "good" or not, whether you feel Him or not, and whether you believe it or not, the Holy Spirit is with you at all times.

Neither you nor I can do the will of the Father without the power of the Holy Spirit. We want to live holy lives, lay hands on the sick, teach, preach, be good husbands and wives, be good parents; but all these things are impossible without the empowerment of the Holy Spirit. It is absolutely vital that we find out who the Holy Spirit is, what He does, and how to connect with Him. Fortunately, we have Jesus' example to guide us; He is the perfect example of a man walking in the full manifestation of the power of the Holy Spirit.

You desperately need the power He brings for every moment of your life; and you need His freedom: ". . . where the Spirit of the Lord is, there is freedom" (2 Cor. 3:17). If you are sick, He will set you free. If you are poor, He can fill your billfold. If you need wisdom for a difficult situation, He is the Spirit of Truth. The Holy Spirit wants to bring liberty to every area of your life.

Once He convinced people to accept the Holy Spirit, then Jesus made Him accessible. He said, "After I die and rise from the dead, I'm not going to leave you here by yourself. I won't leave you like orphans; I'll ask the Father to give you another Comforter." (John 14:16.) It took the Atonement—Jesus' innocence exchanged for our guilt—in order for the Holy Spirit to be accessible to us. Jesus gave His life to give us that access to the Holy Spirit.

In times of emergency, the very first thing we should do is pray in the Spirit. Romans 8:26-27 says, "Likewise the Spirit also helpeth our infirmities: for we know not what we should pray for as we ought: but the Spirit itself maketh intercession for us with groanings which cannot be uttered. And he that searcheth the heart knoweth what is the mind of the Spirit, because he maketh intercession for the saints according to the will of God." The Holy Spirit knows our weaknesses and our infirmities, so He makes intercession for us through our prayer language. He prays a perfect prayer, and God hears His own Spirit as quickly as you hear your own voice when you speak.

How To Commune With the Holy Spirit

Jesus sent the Holy Spirit to us so that we may know Him and *commune* with Him. We need Him to talk to us as we listen and talk back to Him. We can know Him as our close, personal friend.

God is a Spirit, and you were made in His image; so you also have a spirit. In fact, you are a three-fold being: spirit, soul, and body. Your body has five senses—touch, taste, smell, hearing, and feeling. Your soul has a mind, a will, and emotions. Perhaps you have wondered why you have a spirit and what it's for. Your spirit is intended to be the place of residence for the Holy Spirit and the place where you and God talk together. Exodus 33:11 NIV says, "The Lord would speak to Moses face to face, as a man speaks with his friend." This is how the Holy Spirit wants to communicate with you, "as a man speaks with his friend."

The greatest desire of the Holy Spirit is to communicate with you:

> . . . **no one knows the thoughts of God except the Spirit of God. We have not received the spirit of the world but the Spirit who is from God, that we may understand what God has freely given us**
>
> 1 Corinthians 2:11,12 NIV

Some people try to communicate with God through their senses. They want to feel, touch, taste, or smell Him. God sometimes touches your senses, but your flesh isn't designed to communicate with Him.

Some Christians want to communicate with God through their emotions. At times the Holy Spirit will stir your emotions—you may laugh with the joy of the Lord or weep because of the awesomeness of His presence. If, however, your relationship with God is based on your emotions—which can change like the weather—then your Christian experience will be a rollercoaster ride. Your feelings are too unstable to serve as a way to communicate with God.

The greatest temptation for some is to reach out to God with their minds. You are called to keep your mind renewed by the Word. It is always a thrill to get fresh revelation from God's Word, but it would be a mistake to think that revelation knowledge comes *from* your mind instead of *to* your mind from the Holy Spirit. Your mind is where you meet and defeat your adversary, the devil. However, it's too limited to communicate with God. There is only one part of you that can handle the assignment of communicating with God, and that's your spirit: ". . . it is the spirit in a man, the breath of the Almighty, that gives him understanding" (Job 32:8).

First Samuel 10:6 gives us an example of how we get close to Him so He will talk to us:

And the spirit of the Lord will come upon thee, and thou shalt prophesy with them, and shalt be turned into another man.

This passage is speaking about Saul, the man who would become the first king of Israel. The prophet Samuel anointed him, and according to verse 9, God gave Saul a new heart. Look what happened next to Saul:

And when they came thither to the hill, behold, a company of prophets met him; and the spirit of God came upon him, and he prophesied among them.

And it came to pass, when all that knew him before-time saw that, behold, he prophesied among the prophets, then the people said one to another, What is this that is come unto the son of Kish? Is Saul also among the prophets?

1 Samuel 10:10,11

Verse 5 tells us that these prophets whom Saul met were worshiping God. I believe that when Saul met them, he began to join in their singing, and as they worshiped, the spirit of God began to move among them and Saul began to prophesy.

Worship is one of the primary ways to increase your sensitivity to the voice of the Holy Spirit. It is a tool to help you focus your attention on God and cause your problems and desires to fade into the background. Worship is something you *do* not something that happens to you. Sometimes worship can even be a "sacrifice of praise" (Heb. 13:15).

You were created to worship God. He doesn't need your worship, although it pleases Him; but you need to worship Him. Heaven echoes with praise to God, and one day ". . . every knee will bow . . . " in worship to Him (Rom. 14:11). You were created with a *need* for the communion with God that only comes through worship. Worshiping God is communication on the highest level. The Israelites worshiped God. After Moses parted the waters of the Red Sea and led the children of Israel to safety, they praised and worshiped the Lord for their deliverance. Moses and Miriam led the worship, and as they began to sing, dance, and play their instruments in praise to God, the Holy Spirit prophesied through them about the victories God would give them as they took possession of the "promised land." (Ex. 15.)

King David worshiped the Lord too. Of perhaps all the people in the Old Testament, David under-stood, cherished, and delighted in the Holy Spirit the most. After being caught in adultery and murder, David had only one concern: "Please;" he pleaded with God, "don't take your Holy Spirit from me" (Ps. 51.) As a psalmist, David was a master of the art of worship, a singer of praise, and one who reveled in worshiping God. He did not want to lose his sweet communion with the Holy Spirit.

> **Worship is one of the primary ways to increase your sensitivity to the voice of the Holy Spirit.**

Setting the Atmosphere

The psalms were David's way of setting the atmosphere for worship. Praise and worship isn't a song service; it's a way of life. Ephesians 5:19 NIV says, "Speak to one another with psalms, hymns and spiritual songs. Sing and make music in your heart to the Lord." Making music in your heart is the same as singing to yourself. Maybe no one else likes your voice, but God loves it when you sing to Him. Sing to Him in the bathtub, in the shower, when you're fixing your car, and when you're driving. As you keep your spirit open, the Holy Spirit will start talking to you. Make the pledge that David made: "I will bless the Lord at all times: His praise shall continually be in my mouth" (Ps. 34:1 KJV).

An atmosphere of worship opens you up to God.

By worshiping the Lord, you can set an atmosphere for the Holy Spirit to talk to you. Another example of someone who set that atmosphere is the prophet Elisha. King Jehoshaphat of Judah, King Jehoram of Israel, and the king of Edom had gone out in the wilderness to fight the rebelling Moabites. After seven days, they were running out of water and facing an impossible battle. (2 Kings 3.)

King Jehoram said, "God brought us out here just to let us die." But Jehoshaphat said, "No! Surely if we can find a prophet, he can counsel us, because he will have communication with God."

The kings came to Elisha seeking his counsel, and once they presented their case, Elisha stood silently because he had no word to give. He must have thought to himself, *I need a word, I need a word, I need a word!* But he knew exactly what to do. He ordered a harpist to come and play, and while that harpist was worshiping, Elisha got the revelation he needed. He heard from the Holy Spirit.

Worship sets the atmosphere to hear from the Holy Spirit, your Helper. An atmosphere of worship opens you up to God. It takes you out of your mind and into your spirit.

Elisha answered those kings, "You'll have your water and a bonus—you'll also defeat the Moabites." And they did, but only after Elisha set the atmosphere to hear an answer from the Lord.

So far, we've only discussed Old Testament examples. Now let's look at some examples from the New Testament. Colossians 3:16 NIV says:

> **Let the word of Christ dwell in you richly in all wisdom; teaching and admonishing one another in psalms and hymns and spiritual songs, singing with grace in your hearts to the Lord.**

When you begin to sing and worship the Lord, He talks back to you because you're setting an atmosphere for Him to speak.

We need to learn how to live a lifestyle of worship. We should continually let worship lift us up out of our intellect, out of our senses, and into our spirits, so that our spirits can hear from Him.

Spiritual Perception

As you worship God, you will begin to develop spiritual perception. Perception is one of the ways the Holy Spirit will communicate to you. You may not often hear Him with your ears, but you can perceive what He's saying as He whispers truth to your spirit.

Jesus said in Luke 8:46, "Somebody hath touched me: for I *perceive* that virtue is gone out of me." He didn't think or reason it; He perceived it in His spirit through the Holy Spirit.

On another occasion recorded in Luke 9:47, the disciples were arguing about who would be the greatest in the kingdom and Jesus "perceived" the thoughts of their hearts. The Holy Spirit wants to give you perception about people and things in your life.

In Acts 8:23 we find Peter's saying, "I perceive that thou art in the gall of bitterness, and in the bond of iniquity." He was speaking to a sorcerer named Simon. After Simon witnessed some believers receive the baptism of the Holy Spirit, he said to Peter, "I want to buy the power of laying on of hands for people to receive the baptism of the Holy Spirit." (v. 19.) But Peter replied, "I perceive that your heart is wrong." (v. 23.)

The Holy Spirit doesn't always tell you good things about people; sometimes He will show you that a person's motive is wrong and warn you to stay away from him or he may hurt you. Rather than getting all high and mighty, saying, "Peter, you're misjudging me; I'm just in the spirit," Simon the sorcerer said, "Pray for me, that God will have mercy on me." (v. 24.) Peter's spiritual perception brought repentance! So spiritual perception is very important, and we need to be sensitive to listen to the Holy Spirit.

Then again in Acts 14:9-10, we see Paul saying to a man who had never walked, "Stand upright on thy feet." You see, verse 9 tells Paul, "perceiving that he had faith to be healed, said...."

There are times we need to stop and listen, to ask, "God, what are You saying to me?" And if we will listen, we may perceive when someone else has faith and we can join our faith with that person for a miraculous healing.

Opening Your Spirit To Hear

We hear in our spirits and can open our spirits to hear by praying in tongues, or praying in the Spirit. It edifies, rebuilds you, and recharges your battery. When your spirit is built up, you are more open to hear and receive from your Helper.

If you are upset, distressed, or disturbed about a problem, you can pray in the Spirit, and as you do, things begin to happen, because the Bible says the Spirit prays through you:

Likewise the Spirit also helpeth our infirmities: for we know not what we should pray for as we ought: but the Spirit itself maketh intercession for us with groanings which cannot be uttered. And he that searcheth the hearts knoweth what is the mind of the Spirit, because he maketh intercession for the saints according to the will of God. And we know that all things work together for good to them that love God, to them who are the called according to his purpose.

Romans 8:26-28

The Spirit takes you beyond your mind and five physical senses into the Spirit. As you pray in tongues, the inward person of the spirit gets bigger than your soulish person, or your senses, emotion, and intellect.

> There are times we need to stop and listen, to ask, "God, what are You saying to me?"

This verse says He searches the *hearts*—plural. That means the Holy Spirit knows what's in your heart, and what's in the heart of a person with whom you may be involved. Many of the problems we have are people problems. If you're having a problem with someone, you can pray in the Spirit, and the Holy Spirit will search the hearts of those involved and then work things out together for good, according to verse 28.

Praying in the Spirit also opens up your spirit in order for God to work on your heart and bring you in line with what He wants. Many times your mind, emotions, and senses are not in line with God's will, but the Spirit can put you in line if you will follow Him.

Praying in tongues also brings revelation. First Corinthians 2:9,10 says:

Eye hath not seen, nor ear heard, neither have entered into the heart of man, the things which God hath prepared for them that love him. But God hath revealed them unto us by his Spirit: for the Spirit searcheth all things, yea, the deep things of God.

The Spirit takes you beyond your mind and five physical senses into the Spirit.

If you need revelation from God, get into the Spirit by praying in tongues. The reference here in 1 Corinthians 2 tells us about praying in tongues, and to show you that I'm not taking it out of context, let's look at what verses 12 and 13 say:

Now we have received, not the spirit of the world, but the spirit which is of God; that we might know the things that are freely given to us of God. Which things also we speak, not in the words which man's wisdom teacheth, but which the Holy Ghost teacheth; comparing spiritual things with spiritual.

When we start to pray in tongues, we begin to understand the deep things of God. We begin to compare spiritual things with spiritual things. Our spirits begin to open, and we hear what God wants us to do in any given situation. Glory to God!

In the mornings I like to walk and pray. One morning I was praying in the Spirit about something. I just prayed and prayed, thinking, *I really need an answer to this problem,* but I kept praying in the Spirit.

Soon the Lord said to me, *Get two people to agree with you in prayer about this, because a three-fold cord is not easily broken. This will be taken care of.*

YOU CAN KNOW THE ONE JESUS PROMISED

That's the answer—the revelation God gave me after a season of praying in tongues. In fact, everything successful I've ever done usually came after I had a revelation from praying in tongues. It is so powerful!

You might feel like a nut, walking back and forth and praying in tongues. If you are honest, you probably have thought to your-self, *What am I doing walking back and forth praying in tongues? I've been at this for an hour. Why do I keep doing this?* Your head doesn't understand what you're doing, but you can't let your human reasoning come into it; you've got to stay in your spirit. If you begin to reason in your heart, you're not going to perceive in your spirit.

Let me ask you something. Does God answer prayer? Of course He does! Well, does He answer the prayer of the Spirit? Absolutely! Furthermore, He reveals what the Spirit wants to pray through you, *but* it comes from praying in the Spirit.

Remember, we said that getting into the Spirit brings revela-tion. Verse 14 illuminates this fact:

But the natural man receiveth not the things of the Spirit of God: for they are foolishness unto him: neither can he know them, because they are spiritually discerned.

You may say, "Marilyn, I want to hear from the Lord! I want the Holy Spirit to speak to me." Well, start getting into the Spirit, so that you can discern things *spiritually.*

Be Drunk in the Spirit!

Now look at Ephesians 5:18-20. There's something else that happens to you when you start praying in the Spirit:

Be not drunk with wine, wherein is excess; but be filled with the Spirit; speaking to yourselves in psalms and hymns and spiritual songs, singing and making melody in your heart to the Lord; giving thanks always for all things.

When you pray in the Spirit, you get filled. In other words, you get "drunk"—drunk *in the Spirit*. We see this comparison several times in the New Testament. In fact, on the Day of Pentecost, Peter stood before the crowds that had gathered and said, "For these are not drunken, as ye suppose" (Acts 2:15). The newly Spirit-filled believers were drunk in the Spirit!

A person drunk in the natural is often apt to sing and thank everyone for everything! Have you ever noticed that nothing seems to bother a drunk? You can say, "Sit down and quit that drinking!" and the drunken person says, "Okay, thank you so much."

But we're to be drunk in the Spirit—singing and giving thanks to the Lord. It happens because you're not in your mind and you're not in your senses; you're in the Spirit.

Get "drunk"—and stay drunk—in the Holy Spirit and you won't have any trouble doing what the next verse tells you to do: "Be filled [or drunk] with the Spirit...submitting yourselves one to another in the fear of God" (Eph. 5:18,21).

You might say, "Well, if you had to live with the person I'm married to, you couldn't stand it." Maybe you need to get drunk more often—filled with the Spirit. If you watch a drunken person, more than likely he is completely submissive. You can say, "Come here!" and he says, "Okay." He's drunk; he'll do just about anything.

Likewise, getting and staying drunk in the Spirit enables you to submit to God and others.

I had a young man once tell me a story along these lines. He said he had a hard time working. He'd had several different jobs and didn't like his bosses on any of them. In the meantime, he had an idea for a tremendous invention. The only problem was that he didn't have anyone to invest in it so he could build it.

Likewise, getting and staying drunk in the Spirit enables you to submit to God and others.

The young man prayed about it, and God said to him, *How come you never get along with any of your bosses?* When the young man said he didn't know, God said, *I'm going to show you how to treat your boss.*

The man listened to God and began treating his current boss in a godly manner. One day his boss saw the man's invention and said, "Son, I'm going to put you on the map and pay for it. You'll have the funding for your invention!"

When you get in the Spirit, you can submit to a boss, because your Helper, the Holy Spirit, will provide you with the revelation of how to handle the situation. Most of our problems in relationships come because we don't drink enough to stay drunk in the Holy Spirit.

It's easy to come to church and get drunk in the Spirit. We come together and worship, and the Spirit begins to commune with us, but God would like for you to get drunk in the Spirit at home. Somebody who's serious about drinking in the natural has a bottle at home!

You just don't get drunk in the Spirit at church; you take your "bottle" with you. You pray in tongues at home, at work, and everywhere you go. I cannot emphasize how important it is to pray in the Spirit, because that's what keeps your spirit open for Him to communicate with you and you with Him.

As we discussed earlier, we commune with the Holy Spirit through worship, which opens you up to hear from Him, and through prayer in the Spirit, which brings revelation of the deep things of God.

The Free Gift

The Holy Spirit is the promise of the Father which Jesus mentioned in Acts 1:8, right before He ascended into heaven: "But ye shall receive power, after that the Holy Ghost is come upon you."

God did not give the gift of the Holy Spirit on the basis of your works or by "tarrying," or waiting. Simply, we are saved by grace, and we receive the Holy Spirit by grace. People say, "I'm not good enough to receive the Holy Spirit yet." I say it the other way around: You receive the Holy Spirit, and He makes you better.

The Holy Spirit is the Spirit of freedom and liberty. Freedom means to be exempt from obligation, not bound nor charged in any way. A free person is able to act or move at will without restraint. The message of Galatians is spiritual life and freedom in the Holy Spirit. The believers of Galatia had received the Holy Spirit by faith in Jesus Christ. The Holy Spirit freed them from sin and brought these believers into relationship with God. The liberating Holy Spirit had worked miracles among the people, setting them free from spiritual and physical bondage.

You just don't get drunk in the Spirit at church; you take your "bottle" with you.

Nevertheless, the Galatians were being troubled by Jewish taskmasters trying to impose the law upon them. These law keepers saw right relationship with God as something to be earned, instead of the free gift of the Holy Spirit. Their message of works tempted the believers to lose their freedom in the Holy Spirit and come under the yoke of the law. However, it was the Holy Spirit who had birthed them into His life and liberty, and it was the Holy Spirit who would continue to sustain that life in them:

> **Did you receive the Spirit by observing the law, or by believing what you heard? Are you so foolish? After beginning with the Spirit, are you now trying to attain your goal by human effort? Does God give you his Spirit and work miracles among you because you observe the law, or because you believe what you heard?**
>
> **Galatians 3:2,3,5**

As believers we freely receive the Spirit and His gift of eternal life the moment we accept Jesus as Savior. There is absolutely no price we can pay, no work we can ever do, to merit the Holy Spirit in our lives. Freely the Spirit has been given to us as a result of the price Jesus paid. There are "no strings attached."

One time I was teaching in a night service. After the service some young couples came up to me and asked if I could go out for coffee with them. Normally I don't do that, since I didn't know them, but I felt very much in my heart that I was supposed to go. There were about six couples, and they had some Bible questions they wanted to ask me.

One young man said, "I've never been filled with the Spirit. My father's a Spirit-filled pastor, but I've never felt good enough to receive the baptism of the Holy Spirit. Some day I will get good enough, and I will receive. I really want to—I'm really hungry."

I told him that the Bible says you can receive as soon as you ask. He didn't believe me, so I gave him some Scriptures, among them this one:

If ye then, being evil, know how to give good gifts unto your children: how much more shall your heavenly Father give the Holy Spirit to them that ask him?

Luke 11:13

I told him he could be Spirit-filled right there in that restaurant. He said he wouldn't do that right there; he wanted to go out in the parking lot. So we went to the parking lot, and he received the baptism of the Holy Spirit! The Holy Spirit is a gift, and we can receive Him as soon we have faith to do so.

We'll see that in Acts 10. Cornelius and his household didn't "get good enough." They heard the Word—faith comes by hearing the Word, according to Romans 10:17—and they were Spirit-filled.

The Holy Spirit is the One who abides in you and will never leave you. He is a person who is also your guide, your helper, and your aid. He leads you in truth. It is He who will give you revelation that brings you through, makes you win, makes you triumph. The Holy Spirit works in you, speaks to you, deals with you, and communes with you.

Stay fresh in the Holy Spirit! Pray in the Spirit all the time. Embrace and cherish the person of the Holy Spirit, His calling and function in you, and His gifts, which He works through you.

Empowered From on High

First Corinthians 12:1 begins, "Now concerning spiritual gifts, brethren, I would not have you ignorant."

These are *spiritual* gifts. They don't come out of your intellect or education; they come from the Holy Spirit. Furthermore, they are gifts given specifically to the "brethren," or the Body of Christ.

> **Ye know that ye were Gentiles, carried away unto these dumb idols, even as ye were led. Wherefore I give you to understand, that no man speaking by the Spirit of God calleth Jesus accursed: and that no man can say that Jesus is the Lord, but by the Holy Ghost.**
>
> **1 Corinthians 12:2,3**

Paul wrote to the Corinthians as though everyone was spiritually gifted. . . you do not lack any spiritual gift as you eagerly wait for our Lord Jesus Christ to be revealed (1 Cor. 1:7).

Gift in this verse is the Greek word *charisma* which means "a divine gratuity." It is a special gift, freely and graciously given by God to His people. In the context of I Corinthians, we come to discover that these gifts often have to do with the gifts of revelation knowledge like the word of wisdom, word of knowledge, and discernment of spirits.

In terms of the gifts of speech, they are prophecy, tongues, and interpretation of tongues. All are referred to as "gifts of the Spirit." The first 11 chapters of I Corinthians provide revelation about the fruit of the Spirit, which complement the gifts of the Spirit.

Chapters 12-14 of I Corinthians have to do with spiritual gifts. Chapter 12 is broken down into several sections: we are to test spiritual gifts (12:1-3); we are to recognize the common source of these gifts (12:4-11); the Spirit-baptized believers had to have a relationship to the body (chapters 12-20); and there is an order of gifts so that each member of the Body has different assigned duties (chapters 27-31).

The gifts listed in I Corinthians 12:4-12 are also referred to as "spiritual gifts:" They involve the supernatural and exceed the natural, and are freely bestowed on members of the Church by the Spirit. The human spirit cannot generate such gifts. Sometimes they are called the charismatic gifts, from the Greek word, *charisma:*

> **To one there is given through the Spirit the message of wisdom, to another the message of knowledge by means of the same Spirit, to another faith by the same Spirit, to another gifts of healing by that one Spirit, to another miraculous powers, to another prophecy, to another distinguishing between spirits, to another speaking in**

**different kinds of tongues, and to still another the inter-
pretation of tongues.**

1 Corinthians 12:8-10 NIV

Paul tells us there are a variety of gifts and different kinds
of services:

**There are different kinds of gifts, but the same Spirit.
There are different kinds of service, but the same Lord.
There are different kinds of working, but the same God
works all of them in all men.**

1 Corinthians 12:4-6 NIV

Even though there are diversities of operations, effects, or ener-
gies, their manifestations reveal their nature-all of them are for the
common good, for the benefit of others, and for everyone's profit:

**Now to each one the manifestation of the Spirit is
given for the common good.**

1 Corinthians 12:7 NIV

These gifts have great purposes. They manifest the power of
God; help carry out the great commission of Jesus; edify and
perfect the church; and bring deliverance to God's people. They
are easily broken down into categories. There are three spoken
gifts: prophecy, diverse tongues, and the interpretation of tongues;
three revelation gifts: the word of knowledge, the word of wisdom,
and discerning of spirits; and three power gifts: faith, working
of miracles, and the gifts of healing. The gifts are given as the
Spirit wills.

The baptism of the Holy Spirit sets the Church on fire, empowering them to become witnesses to Christ's resurrection. Therefore,
signs and wonders are to follow believers who are filled with the
Holy Spirit.

The Holy Spirit doesn't flow through everyone the same way. I once saw a woman on a bus in China extend her hand out the window to lay hands on and pray for a handicapped woman. As she did, the handicapped woman set her crutch down! Now, that's an unusual situation, but that's how the gifts of healing flowed through this particular woman.

The key is that the manifestations of the gifts are to profit other people.

We may sometimes see people operate in the gifts in a way we don't always understand, because there *are* differences in operations and administrations. The key, according to verse 7, is that the manifestations of the gifts are to profit other people: "The manifestation of the Spirit is given to every man to profit withal."

In one of our meetings, we had a woman in her late thirties who had been deaf in her right ear since she was a child. God healed her during the service, and she was able to hear perfectly. Don't you think she found that profitable? When the gifts are in operation, people profit from them; they're edified, blessed, changed, and transformed because of the Holy Spirit's moving.

Now let's examine the gifts closely.

There are nine gifts of the Spirit, and in order to remember them, I like to divide them into the three D's—discerning gifts, dynamic gifts, and declaring gifts.

First are the three discerning gifts: the word of knowledge, the word of wisdom, and the discerning of spirits. These are revelation gifts having to do with your mind.

Through these gifts, the Holy Spirit unveils Himself as the Spirit of Discernment. Nehemiah and the Israelites who assisted him in rebuilding the temple's walls were faced with intense opposition. When Sanballat and Tobiah realized they could not frighten the Israelites to stop building, or persuade the king to stop the work of God, they conspired to kill Nehemiah. What Sanballat and Tobiah didn't understand, however, was the omniscience of Israel's God. He knew of the death plot against Nehemiah, and the Holy Spirit opened Nehemiah's spiritual understanding to discern the motive of the heart of Shemaiah, the false prophet:

> But I said, "Should a man like me run away? Or should one like me go into the temple to save his life? I will not go!" I realized that God had not sent him, but that he had prophesied against me because Tobiah and Sanballat had hired him.

> Nehemiah 6:11,12 NIV

Not only do New Testament believers have the indwelling of the Holy Spirit, but we also have His gifts operating in us and are fully equipped to meet the challenges Satan or people put in our way. (1 Cor. 12:7-11.)

Next are the three dynamic gifts: the gift of healing, the working of miracles, and faith. These have more to do with the physical body. The last three are the declaring gifts: prophecy, diverse kinds of tongues, and interpretation of tongues. These have to do with telling something to the Body of Christ.

Now, the gifts do something very special. They bring unity in the Body, according to verse 13:

> For by one Spirit are we all baptized into one body, whether we be Jews or Gentiles, whether we be bond or free; and have been all made to drink into one Spirit.

HE WILL GIVE YOU ANOTHER HELPER

When we are baptized in the Holy Spirit, we all get the same "drink." Some drink more than others and some get more drunk than others—but we all drink of the same Spirit. So the operation of the gifts brings unity to the Body of Christ.

The Gifts of the Spirit in Action

The book of Acts gives us several examples of the gifts of the Spirit in action. In Acts 6, the apostles were having a real problem. Some of the people in the church were not being fed. It looked like they might run into strife or contention in the church over who should leave the ministry and serve the people.

> **The operation of the gifts brings unity to the Body of Christ.**

This may sound like a simple thing, but nothing can cause the split of a church faster than strife among its members. The cause of the problem was between the Jews of the dispersion who spoke the Greek language of their homelands and the Hebrew-speaking Jews who lived in Israel. The Grecian Jews felt that their widows were being shortchanged when provisions were distributed commonly among the believers.

I love how God resolved this potentially church-splitting issue. I believe He gave them a word of wisdom for the situation and showed them what to do.

> **Then the twelve called the multitude of the disciples unto them, and said, It is not reason that we should leave the word of God, and serve tables. Wherefore, brethren, look ye out among you seven men. . . .**
>
> **Acts 6:2,3**

The disciples were told to find certain men with the qualifications to handle the situation:

> **...men of honest report, full of the Holy Ghost and wisdom.**
>
> **Acts 6:3**

It was the apostles' decision to delegate the work of serving tables, but the multitude of disciples were given the task of finding the right men to do the job. Once they found the right men, the apostles ordained them through the laying on of hands:

> **And the saying pleased the whole multitude: and they chose Stephen, a man full of faith and of the Holy Ghost, and Philip, and Prochorus, and Nicanor, and Timon, and Parmenas, and Nicolas a proselyte of Antioch: whom they set before the apostles: and when they had prayed, they laid their hands on them.**
>
> **Acts 6:5,6**

These men were the first deacons of the Church. *Deacon* comes from the Greek word *diakonia*, which means "servant or aid."[3] A deacon, then, is someone who lends a hand where help is needed.

Now, that word of wisdom to the apostles was the key, the perfect word for the situation, and the Holy Spirit helped the Church survive another attempt to put out its flaming testimony. The result was a brighter fire:

> **And the word of God increased; and the number of the disciples multiplied in Jerusalem greatly.... And Stephen, full of faith and power, did great wonders and miracles among the people.**
>
> **Acts 6:7,8**

Opposition only serves to make the Church stronger! God, by His Spirit in men, is able to overcome every obstacle or roadblock that Satan tries to erect against the Lord's burning bush; this gospel flame is eternal! Notice that by now even the priests were being swept along in this Holy Spirit revival:

> . . . and a great company of the priests were obedient to the faith.
>
> **Acts 6:7**

All this took place because of the gifts of the Spirit operating through the disciples. Let me tell you—the gifts are not just for church. They are for our lifestyles, our homes, and our families. You may have a child you don't know what to do with. The Holy Spirit can give you a word of wisdom and help you turn him or her in the right direction.

Acts 7 recounts another instance of the gifts in action. The apostle Stephen had a word of knowledge to the Jewish leaders. "You resist the Holy Spirit," he told them after he'd preached Christ to them. (v. 51.)

How do we know that his saying this was a word of knowledge? The Bible tells us Stephen was in the Spirit:

> **He, being full of the Holy Ghost, looked up stedfastly into heaven, and saw the glory of God, and Jesus standing on the right hand of God.**
>
> **Acts 7:55**

As the Jews stoned him, Stephen cried, "Lord, lay not this sin to their charge" (v. 60).

Clearly, Stephen spoke a word of knowledge because it exposed the Jews' hearts, and made them angry, but the word penetrated the heart of a certain man that was standing by in a powerful way. His name was Saul, the man who would later become the mighty apostle Paul.

Truly, a believer's operation in the gifts of the Spirit reaps much fruit. Now, these have both been cases of words of wisdom and words of knowledge. Acts 5 gives us an example of discerning of spirits.

> **A certain man named Ananias, with Sapphira his wife, sold a possession, and kept back part of the price, his wife also being privy to it, and brought a certain part, and laid it at the apostles' feet.**
>
> **Acts 5:1,2**

In order to understand the sin of Ananias and Sapphira, we have to back up to Acts 4:34-35, which speak about believers in the early church:

> **Neither was there any among them that lacked: for as many as were possessors of lands or houses sold them, and brought the prices of the things that were sold, and laid them down at the apostles' feet: and distribution was made unto every man according as he had need.**

Those who sold their land or houses brought the proceeds (as much or as little as they felt led to give) as *freewill offerings* to the apostles for distribution to the needy.

Accordingly, when Ananias and Sapphira presented the money from the sale of their property, Peter said, "You have lied to the Holy Spirit. You sold your property and kept back part of the price." (Acts 5:3.) When Ananias heard this, he immediately fell down dead.

Later, when his wife came before Peter, he questioned her about the price of the land. She didn't know what had happened to her husband, and she said, "Yea, for so much" (v. 8).

Peter answered, "No, that's not what it was. Your husband lied to the Holy Spirit, and we just carried his body out. You lied, and we're going to carry your body out too." (v. 9.) And just as Peter had said, Sapphira fell down dead. Peter knew this by the discerning of spirits.

This was the Church's first sin. Now, many people think that money is the root of all evil and that the sin here is about money; the Bible doesn't say that! It is the *love* of money that is said to be the root of all evil. (1 Tim. 6:10.) It is only when we divorce money from sense that sin deadens our conscience and dulls our spiritual lives.

It was not a sin for Ananias and Sapphira to own land, neither to sell it, nor to keep any or all of the money from the sale of that land. It is true that when God touches our hearts, He often touches our checkbooks as well. Ananias and Sapphira, in contrast, gave out of greed—not for money, but for reputation. They lied about the *amount* given so that they would appear more generous than what was legitimately so. Theirs was the sin of hypocrisy.

There are five sins in the New Testament said to be sins against the Holy Spirit.

1. Resisting the Holy Spirit:

> **Ye stiffnecked and uncircumcised in heart and ears, ye do always resist the Holy Ghost: as your fathers did, so do ye (Acts 7:51).**

2. Blasphemy against the Holy Spirit:

> **Wherefore I say unto you, All manner of sin and blasphemy shall be forgiven unto men: but the blas-**

phemy against the Holy Ghost shall not be forgiven unto men (Matt. 12:31).

3. Grieving the Holy Spirit:

   And grieve not the holy Spirit of God, whereby ye are sealed unto the day of redemption (Eph. 4:30).

4. Quenching the Holy Spirit:

   Quench not the Spirit (1 Thess. 5:19).

5. Lying to the Holy Spirit:

   But Peter said, Ananias, why hath Satan filled thine heart to lie to the Holy Ghost, and to keep back part of the price of the land? (Acts 5:3).

The result of this one lie was death. Peter was not the disciplinarian, but the Holy Spirit revealed the truth to Peter and the discipline came from God:

> ...thou hast not lied unto men, but unto God. And Ananias hearing these words fell down, and gave up the ghost. . . .
>
> Acts 5:4,5

In His mercy, God does not immediately judge everyone who sins. The deaths of Ananias and Sapphira served as a warning to others in the early Church. Luke tells us twice the result of this divine discipline:

> . . . and great fear came on all them that heard these things.
>
> Acts 5:5

> . . . and great fear came upon all the church, and upon as many as heard these things.
>
> Acts 5:11

Though God judged the sin, He gave Peter discernment of the sin by the Holy Spirit, his Helper.

Now, so far we've looked at gifts, which have operated through great men of God. The gifts operate through ordinary people too. You don't have to be an Oral Roberts or Kathryn Khulman for the gifts to operate through you. Acts 8 tells us about an ordinary man, Philip the deacon who waited on tables.

The gifts operate through ordinary people too.

Philip had a burden for Samaria, so he went there and preached, and although he wasn't a preacher but a layperson, Samaria experienced some of the most unusual miracles. This is the same man whom God later caught by the Spirit and transported to another place to preach. (v. 39.)

God worked the gift of miracles through an ordinary person—Philip—and that's what He wants to do through us today.

Paul operated in this gift when he was on board a ship as a prisoner and they were caught in a storm. (Acts 27.) It looked like the ship was about to go down, but Paul announced before the crew:

> Now I exhort you to be of good cheer: for there shall be no loss of any man's life among you, but of the ship. For there stood by me this night the angel of God, whose I am, and whom I serve, saying, Fear not, Paul; thou must be brought before Caesar: and, lo, God hath given thee all them that sail with thee.
>
> Wherefore, sirs, be of good cheer: for I believe God, that it shall be even as it was told me.
>
> **Acts 27:22-25**

Paul moved in the gift of faith, and just as God had promised, everyone was saved.

You may say, "I'm in a dark crisis; I'm going through a terrible thing." The gift of faith can take you through a crisis. Everything can be falling apart on you, and you can be thinking, *Isn't this wonderful? God's going to do the biggest miracle I've ever experienced!*

The gift of healing is just as potent. Consider the beggar in Acts 3. Crippled from birth, he had *never* known physical wholeness. He was convinced that no remedy could overcome his disability, so all his life, he did the "logical" thing; he begged for money. When Peter and John walked by, he didn't ask to be healed; he asked for money. He didn't recognize the gift of healing that was available to turn his life around.

Peter and John did, however. As the man begged, they looked straight at him—and straight into the heart of the matter. Filled with the Holy Spirit, they were able to address the *real need.*

> **Peter said, Look at us!...Silver and gold (money) I do not have; but what I do have, that I give to you: in [the use of] the name of Jesus Christ of Nazareth, walk! ...And at once his feet and ankle bones became strong and steady. And leaping forth he stood and began to walk.... The people...recognized him as the man who usually sat [begging] for alms...and they were filled with wonder and amazement.... Peter, seeing it, answered the people...Why are you so surprised and wondering at this? ...by faith in His name, has made this man whom you see and recognize well and strong. [Yes] the faith which is through and by Him [Jesus] has given the man this perfect soundness [of body] before all of you.**
>
> **Acts 3:4,6-10,12,16** AMP

However severe a physical ailment may be, it is no match for the healing power of God!

We can see the gift of prophecy operating in a man named Agabus. Acts 11:28-30 tells us he prophesied of a dearth, or a famine, coming. He said, "There's going to be a famine, so we need to get ready to feed the saints."

When the famine hit, Christians didn't suffer, because God showed by the Spirit through prophecy what was to come. They were prepared. The Spirit can tell you through prophecy—and also through tongues and interpretation—what's to come, and when the situation comes, you can be the winner in it.

The gifts of the Spirit are to be a powerful witness of God's power to unbelievers.

God wants you to operate supernaturally through the gifts of the Spirit. We will explore in the next chapter how the gifts of the Spirit work with the fruits of the Spirit to bring about God's plan in your life.

The gifts of the Spirit are to be a powerful witness of God's power to unbelievers. You don't have to be some "big name" to operate in them; God uses ordinary people to perform signs and wonders.

Covet the gifts of the Spirit. Become a willing vessel and God will use you!

Chapter 3

The Fruit of the Holy Spirit

*H*ave you ever been to an orchard in the springtime? Everything seems so peaceful. There's a fresh, sweet smell in the air, bees are everywhere, and there's a hope of better things to come in just a few short months. Yet, if you look behind the scenes, you will see the husbandman busy at his task of preparing for the coming harvest; he knows that if he just sits by and does nothing, his harvest will be small. So under his care, the ground will be cultivated and fertilized to provide nourishment for the trees; branches will be pruned regularly; and anything that comes against the trees, such as bugs or worms, will be dealt with immediately.

Finally, the harvest comes and he picks the fruit his efforts have produced—ripe, luscious fruit—which I'm sure he is the first one to sample. His hard work, patience, perseverance, and persistence have paid off in a wonderfully sweet bounty, which he can then sell for others to enjoy as well.

The Holy Spirit expects to see evidence of His hard work in the lives of Christians.

In much the same way, the Holy Spirit expects to see evidence of His hard work in the lives of Christians. That evidence is then the proof that we are who we say we are—followers of Christ—and is often referred to as "the fruit of the Spirit." It is aptly called this, for it is only under the care of the Holy Spirit that the Christian will bear fruit.

Jesus even told us that He was the vine (tree) from which we, the branches, are to bear fruit. Now, while Jesus is the Vine, the Holy Spirit is the living "sap" in the Vine that runs through the branches, nourishing them, and eventually producing fruit:

> "I [Jesus] **am the vine; you are the branches. If a man remains in me and I in him, he will bear much fruit; apart from me you can do nothing.**"
>
> **John 15:5** NIV

The Nature of Fruit

As we have already seen, the Holy Spirit if the source of all life. Every living thing was created through His life-giving power. What is even more awe-inspiring is that every living thing He created has within itself the ability to produce life after its own kind—from the lowest microscopic amoeba and protozoa to the largest and most complicated forms of plant and animal life. Most life reproduces by bearing "fruit"; this fruit is a miniature of the parent and eventually grows and matures until it is capable of reproducing as well.

Nonetheless, when we think of fruit, we usually think of the edible kind that grows on vines or trees. Interestingly enough, although the leaves and the fruit give the tree a very attractive appearance, the tree has no use for its own fruit. Even the leaves of the tree are involved in sustaining the life of the tree, but not the fruit. Yes, the seed in the fruit will produce another tree, but the tree cannot use the fruit. Rather, the fruit sustains life for those who eat it. Therein lies the tree's value.

Jesus, the physical fruit of the Spirit, is also the living Word, and we must ingest the Word of God into our spirits in order to have His life. The Word of God is food for our spirits, continually sustaining our spiritual life. In fact, Jesus said unless we eat His flesh and drink His blood, we have no part with Him; our new Spirit-filled lives can only be obtained through the blood of Jesus:

> **Jesus said to them, "I tell you the truth, unless you eat the flesh of the Son of Man and drink his blood, you have no life in you. Whoever eats my flesh and drinks my blood has eternal life, and I will raise him up at the last day".**
>
> **John 6:53,54** NIV

Another very interesting comparison can be drawn between the value of a tree being in its fruit, and God receiving glory because we are bearing His fruit:

> **In love he [God] predestined us to be adopted as his sons through Jesus Christ, in accordance with his pleasure and will—to the praise of his glorious grace, . . . in conformity with the purpose of his will, in order that we . . . might be for the *praise of his glory.*"**
>
> **Ephesians. 1:4-6,11,12** NIV

Our value as Christians is seen in the fruit we produce.

It is only after spiritual rebirth that we can produce the characteristics of Jesus Christ, who now indwells our spirits, and who always sought to do the will of the Father and bring glory to His Father. Likewise, our value as Christians is seen in the fruit we produce: "The fruit of the righteous is a tree of life, . . . " (Prov. 11:30). When we lead someone to the Lord, we aren't just yielding fruit, we're planting trees of righteousness that in turn will go and produce after their own kind.

The Holy Spirit Produced Jesus

As is to be expected, the One who produced all life also produces fruit. The first physical fruit produced by the Holy Spirit was Jesus Christ, God's Son come to earth in the flesh. Jesus was the exact likeness of His unseen Father. He was the "first fruit," and Christians are the harvest of fruit, which has followed.

Jesus died for our sins and, as God's Seed, was then "planted" in the ground so He could rise as the "first born" from the dead:

> **I tell you the truth, unless a kernel of wheat falls to the ground and dies, it remains only a single seed. But if it dies, it produces many seeds.**
>
> **John 12:24**

Truly, the Seed from Calvary's tree has produced much fruit.

The Fruit of the Flesh

When Adam "sold out" to Satan for a bite of fruit, that fruit contained a seed which produced death in him and all his offspring. Adam and Eve were cut off from God, their relationship severed with their Creator. Instead, Satan became the inspiration (father) of their fallen nature. They and the fruit of their bodies would now reproduce after the nature of sin:

> **The acts of the sinful nature are obvious: sexual immorality, impurity and debauchery; idolatry and witchcraft; hatred, discord, jealousy, fits of rage, selfish ambition, dissensions, factions and envy; drunkenness, orgies, and the like . . . those who live like this will not inherit the kingdom of God.**
>
> Galatians 5:19-21 NIV

As long as man is in the flesh, he has to deal with the flesh nature, which strives to produce fruit after its own kind. But God in His infinite mercy and love made a way for Adam and his seed to be delivered from the flesh nature and restored to fellowship with Him through His Seed, Jesus:

> **Who will rescue me from this body of death? Thanks be to God—through Jesus Christ our Lord! So then, I myself in my mind am a slave to God's law, but in the sinful nature a slave to the law of sin. Therefore, there is now no condemnation for those who are in Christ Jesus, because through Christ Jesus the** *law of the Spirit of life* **set me free from the law of sin and death.**
>
> Romans 7:24,25; 8:1,2 NIV

Therefore, I urge you, brothers, in view of God's mercy, to offer your bodies as living sacrifices, holy and pleasing to God-this is your spiritual act of worship. Do not conform any longer to the pattern of this world, but be transformed by the renewing of your mind. Then you will be able to test and approve what God's will is-his good, pleasing and perfect will.

Romans 12:1,2 NIV

Live by the Spirit, and you will not gratify the desires of the sinful nature. For the sinful nature desires what is contrary to the Spirit, and the Spirit what is contrary to the sinful nature. They are in conflict with each other, so that you do not do what you want. But if you are led by the Spirit, you are not under law.

Galatians 5:16-18 NIV

> When we are in fellowship with God through communication with the Holy Spirit—who has made our spirit nature alive to God— we overcome the nature of the flesh.

When we "eat" of Jesus, that Seed produces a new nature in our inner man. When we are in fellowship with God through communication with the Holy Spirit—who has made our spirit nature alive to God—we overcome the nature of the flesh. Instead of producing the fruit of the flesh, we produce the fruit of the Holy Spirit.

The Fruit of the Spirit

The Holy Spirit, who lives in all born-again Christians, reproduces fruit in their lives that is after God's kind—miniatures of Himself and of Jesus. Therefore, the fruit of the Holy Spirit in a believer's life is spiritual fruit, not physical fruit. The Spirit's fruit in us cannot be seen, but it can certainly be enjoyed. What is this fruit? Galatians 5:22-23 NIV tells us:

The fruit of the Spirit is love, joy, peace, patience, kindness, goodness, faithfulness, gentleness and self control. Against such things there is no law.

Now let me take a moment to stress a very important point. God has not called us to examine the evidence of fruit in *other's* lives. He has called us to produce fruit in *our own lives.*

I also want to make it clear that on any occasion, the gifts of the Holy Spirit can flow together with any of the fruit. By pairing a gift with a fruit, according to the order in which they are listed in the Bible, you can see how they work together in the lives of believers. You can also see how a person must walk in love and at the same time move in the power of the Holy Spirit.

First Corinthians 12:8-10 lists the gifts of the Spirit, while Galatians lists the fruit of the born-again Christian. Here's how they match up so you can see how they should operate.

Fruit of the Spirit	Gifts of the Spirit
Love	The message of wisdom
Joy	The message of knowledge
Peace	Faith
Patience	Gifts of healing
Kindness	Miraculous powers
Goodness	Prophecy
Faithfulness	Distinguishing between spirits
Gentleness	Tongues
Self-control	Interpretation of tongues

God's love is a choice and not an emotion.

I want to examine the fruit of the Spirit in light of the nine gifts of the Spirit. After Paul listed the gifts of the Spirit in 1 Corinthians 12, he went on in chapter 13 to emphasize that these gifts must always be used in love. Then in chapter 14 he explained the regulation of these gifts in operation. With that in mind, let's look at each fruit of the Spirit along with its match in the gifts of the Spirit.

Love—the Message of Wisdom

The love, which the Holy Spirit produces, is the very heart of God's nature, which motivates all His actions. The Greek word for this God-kind of love is *agape,* which means "affection, benevolence; a love-feast; charity." This love is not self-seeking but always considers others before self. True love agrees with the immeasurable value God places on each individual and is the foundation and basis for all the other gifts of the Holy Spirit.

God's love is, first of all, a choice and not an emotion. The fruit of love produces actions for the benefit of another. Although love is lavish, love is *never* indulgent. Love that is genuine must be given away, but it will always produce a rich harvest in return. When we are devoted to God and love Him with all our hearts, the Holy Spirit will produce the fruit of love in our lives:

> **"'Love the Lord your God with all your heart and with all your soul and with all your strength and with all your mind,' and, "Love your neighbor as yourself."**

> **Luke 10:27 NIV**

Love is patient, love is kind. It does not envy, it does not boast, it is not proud. It is not rude, it is not self-seeking, it is not easily angered, it keeps no record of wrongs. Love does not delight in evil but rejoices with the truth. It always protects, always trusts, always hopes, always perseveres. Love never fails.

1 Corinthians 13:4-8 NIV

How great is the love the Father has lavished on us, that we should be called children of God!

God is love. Whoever lives in love lives in God, and God in him.

We love because he first loved us.

1 John 3:1; 4:16,19 NIV

When someone gives a message of wisdom, it is not natural wisdom but a segment of God's wisdom given for a special occasion. If it is truly a revelation from God, love will always flow with it.

When we compare this *agape* fruit with the message of wisdom, Ephesians 4:15 is made clear to us; if someone gives a word of wisdom without "speaking the truth in love," it irritates the Body of Christ. A word of wisdom spoken in an ugly or hateful way sounds like tinkling cymbals and clanging brass. (1 Cor. 13:1.) A message of wisdom must have the fruit of love to make it pure.

Second Kings 5:10-14 provides a beautiful example of a message of wisdom, spoken in love and followed by action. Elisha told a leper, Naaman, to dip in the Jordan River seven times to be healed of his leprosy. When Naaman obeyed, he was healed.

Joy—the Message of Knowledge

Joy is a powerful force born of the Spirit. Joy is the emotion of the Holy Spirit in the human spirit. It is not dependent on the circumstances of life, but it is dependent on God. The joy of the Lord is our strength, and it will sustain us in every situation:

Consider it pure joy, my brothers, whenever you face trials of many kinds, because you know that the testing of your faith develops perseverance. Perseverance must finish its work so that you may be mature and complete, not lacking anything.

James 1:2-4 NIV

> **The action of joy is evidenced in rejoicing and praising God out of a grateful heart.**

The action of joy is evidenced in rejoicing and praising God out of a grateful heart. Paul tells us to rejoice in the Lord always! (Phil. 4:4.) Paul even referred to the Thessalonian Christians as his joy: ". . . you are our glory and joy" (1 Thess. 4:6); and Solomon said, "The prospect of the righteous is joy. . . ." (Prov. 10:28). Joy is woven throughout Jesus' life, and He talked a lot about rejoicing:

If you obey my commands, you will remain in my love, . . . I have told you this so that my joy may be in you and that your joy may be complete

John 15:10,11

Christians should always rejoice, because just knowing Jesus brings great joy:

Though you have not seen him [Jesus], you love him; and even though you do not see him now, you believe in him and are filled with an inexpressible and glorious joy

1 Peter 1:8 NIV

The second gift is the message of knowledge. It reveals a fact unknown to man's natural mind. I don't think it's a coincidence that joy is paired with knowledge. When someone gives you a message of knowledge, it brings joy to your spirit. When it is proclaimed in a church service, it brings joy to the Body of Christ.

In 2 Kings 6:8-23, the prophet Elisha received a message of knowledge regarding the whereabouts of the Syrian army. Elisha would then warn the king of Israel. The king of Aram thought he had a spy among his ranks, when one of his men told him it was Elisha. The Syrian then ordered his men to surround the city of Dothan where Elisha was staying.

When morning came, Elisha's servant was frightened by the sight of the Syrian army encamped about the city. Elisha asked God to open his servant's eyes so he could see in the spiritual realm. The Lord allowed the servant to see an army of angels encamped about the Syrian army that brought him great joy! The word of knowledge gave joy and dispelled fear at the same time.

Peace——Faith

The fruit of peace always prevails with the gift of faith. Remember when Jesus spoke to the winds and waves and said, "Peace, be still"? Immediately the storm ceased and peace was brought to the situation. In the same way, when you see faith moving, your spirit becomes peaceful:

> May the God of hope fill you with all joy and peace
> as you trust in him, so that you may overflow with hope
> by the power of the Holy Spirit
>
> **Romans 15:13** NIV

The peace, which is a fruit of the Spirit, is a tranquil state of mind and heart that cannot be shaken by life's circumstances. The peace of the Spirit protects our hearts and minds, defuses fear and anxiety, and produces a contented heart and a clear mind:

> You [God] will keep in perfect peace him whose mind
> is steadfast, because he trusts in you.
>
> **Isaiah 26:3** NIV

> Do not be anxious about anything, but in everything,
> by prayer and petition, with thanksgiving, present your
> requests to God. And the peace of God, which tran-
> scends all understanding, will guard your hearts and
> your minds in Christ Jesus.
>
> **Philippians 4:6,7** NIV

> But the wisdom that comes from heaven is first of all
> pure;then peace-loving. . . . Peacemakers who sow in
> peace raise a harvest of righteousness.
>
> **James 3:17,18** NIV

When you do not act in faith, you can become fearful for fear is the opposite of faith. When we are afraid, it's hard to exercise our faith. God, who operates on faith, is then unable to work on our behalf. No wonder so many people love to hear faith teaching. It brings peace to their spirits:

> 'Peace I [Jesus] leave with you; my peace I give you. I
> do not give to you as the world gives. Do not let your
> hearts be troubled and do not be afraid.'
>
> **John 14:27** NIV

There are basically three kinds of faith. Romans 12:3 tells us about the first kind: everyone is born with a God-given measure of faith to be saved. Second, hearing the Word of God can increase faith. And third, there is the gift of faith for special occasions. If you've ever found yourself in a crisis where you used your faith for an answer, you've experienced this kind of faith. You didn't prepare for it; it just seemed to drop into your heart.

If you're living in faith, you're living in peace. Faith in God's Word will bring peace to your situation. As peace comes into your life, it will flow out to others around you.

Patience—Gifts of Healing

Patience is the same word as "longsuffering," which is used in the *King James Version*. The Greek word literally means, "long-tempered." Vine's *An Expository Dictionary of New Testament Words* tells us longsuffering "is that quality of self-restraint in the face of provocation which does not hastily retaliate or promptly punish; it is the opposite of anger, and is associated with mercy, and is used of God. Patience is the quality that does not surrender to circumstances or succumb under trial; it is the opposite of despondency and is associated with hope; it is not used of God."

Some people "put up" with such things as sickness or poverty, but that is not in accordance with God's Word: "Beloved, I wish above all things that thou mayest prosper and be in health, even as thy soul prospereth" (3 John 2).

This is why the fruit of patience goes along with gifts of healing, because not all healings are instantaneous. In fact, healing can be an "inherited" promise: "We do not want you to become lazy, but to imitate those who through faith and patience inherit what has been promised . . . . Let us throw off everything that hinders and the sin that so easily entangles, and let us run with perseverance the race marked out for us" (Heb. 6:12; 12:1 NIV).

Healing is not just confined to sickness. In the Old Testament, healing meant "to mend, sow, or repair." So when the Spirit of the Lord is healing someone in his body, He's mending his body. But the Holy Spirit can also mend or repair relationships, habits, memories, or even our nation!

Healing is not just confined to sickness.

The basis for mending relationships is patience, because it can bring about forgiveness: "A man's wisdom gives him patience; it is to his glory to overlook an offense" (Prov. 19:11). It is the basis of humility (Ecc. 7:8), good personal relationships (Prov. 25:15), true wisdom (see Prov. 14:29), and true power (Prov. 16:32); it is also the foundation of eternal fellowship: "Be patient... until the Lord's coming. See how the farmer waits for the land to yield its valuable crop and how patient he is for the autumn and spring rains. You too, be patient and stand firm, because the Lord's coming is near" (James 5:7,8 NIV).

Kindness—Miraculous Powers

Any act to benefit another individual is an act of kindness. The Holy Spirit produces a desire in our hearts to act benevolently toward one another. Kindness would never seek to hurt anyone, but instead, kindness will behave virtuously toward others.

The kindest act in all of history was that of God's sending His only Son, Jesus, to a sinful and lost world. God has given us life through the Holy Spirit and poured upon us His benevolent grace by virtue of the Holy Spirit: ". . . with everlasting kindness I will have compassion on you,' says the Lord your Redeemer" (Isa. 54:8).

And God raised us up with Christ and seated us with him in the heavenly realms in Christ Jesus, in order that in the coming ages he might show the incomparable riches of his grace, *expressed in his kindness to us in Christ Jesus*

Ephesians 2:6,7 NIV

The Spirit produces the fruit of His kindness in our lives, so we are able to extend His kindness to others. Scripture gives us a lot of reasons to be kind. For example, a kind word can cheer someone (Prov. 12:25); being kind to the needy brings blessings (Prov. 14:21) and honors God (Prov. 14:31). Furthermore, a kind man benefits himself (Prov. 11:17).

God has given us life through the Holy Spirit.

Paralleling the fruit of kindness is the gift of miraculous powers. The word powers implies exploding manifestations of God's power. A good example is found in Acts 8:5-24, where Philip was performing such mighty miracles that a man named Simon tried to buy the baptism in the Spirit so he could have the same explosive power Philip was exercising.

During Jesus' ministry on earth, we see a man motivated by kindness and gentleness. Jesus took pity on those who were afflicted and worked wonderful, powerful miracles that still speak to us down through the ages. When Jesus raised Lazarus, the widow's son, Jairus' daughter, and others from the dead; turned water into wine; healed the sick, lame, blind, deaf, and dumb; and forgave sins, His kindness showed through the miraculous results.

I tell you the truth, anyone who has faith in me will do what I have been doing. He will do even greater things than these, because I am going to the Father .

John 14:12 NIV

Therefore, as God's chosen people, holy and dearly loved, clothe yourselves with compassion, kindness . . .

Colossians 3:12 NIV

Goodness—Prophecy

Anything good is useful, virtuous, valuable, excellent, appropriate, or productive. Goodness is the act of well-doing. The Spirit's fruit of goodness produces in believers a life of excellence and virtue, which is true to the nature of the Holy Spirit. In acts of goodness, we make ourselves useful and valuable to others. Whatever we do "out of the goodness of our hearts," or whatever we sow to the Spirit, will reap a harvest:

. . . the one who sows to please the Spirit, from the Spirit will reap eternal life. Let us not become weary in doing good, for at the proper time we will reap a harvest if we do not give up. Therefore, as we have opportunity, let us do good to all people, especially to those who belong to the family of believers

Galatians 6:8-10 NIV

It's not surprising that goodness is paired with prophecy, because the Bible tells us that prophecy must edify, exhort, and comfort people:

But everyone who prophesies speaks to men for their strengthening, encouragement and comfort . . . . he who prophesies edifies the church

1 Corinthians 14:3,4 NIV

When prophecy occurs the way it should, it brings forth goodness. Scripture indicates that in the last days, a lot of goodness will be produced because prophecy will be prevalent. "In the last days, God says, I will pour out my Spirit on all people. Your sons and daughters will prophesy . . ." (Acts 2:17 NIV).

A person who prophesies must be a hearer of the Word. Prophecy should never come from people who don't study the Word. Proverbs 21:28 warns that a false witness will perish. So if you honestly desire to prophesy, get into the Word. God will quicken the Word because you are constantly feeding on it. In fact, when God called Ezekiel to minister as a prophet, He had him eat the Word. (Ezek. 3:1,2.)

It is also important to be an eater of the Word because otherwise you will not be able to judge whether the prophecy is scriptural. If it doesn't line up with the Word, then it's not of God.

There are nine principles for judging prophecy:

1. Prophecy should comfort, edify, or exhort. (1 Cor. 14:3.)

2. True prophecy will always agree with the Word. (Deut. 4:2; Prov. 30:5,6; Isa. 8:19,20; and 2 Tim. 3:16.)

3. True prophecy will always exalt Jesus. (John 16:13-15.)

4. True prophecy will always produce fruit in the character of believers. (Rom. 14:17.)

5. Predictive prophecy should come to pass. (Deut.13:1-5.)

6. If any prophecy promotes disobedience to God's Word, it is not from God. (Deut. 13:1-5.)

7. True prophecy of the Holy Spirit promotes liberty not bondage or spiritual dictatorship. (Rom. 8:15.)

8. True prophecy will inject fresh life. (2 Cor. 3:6.)

9. True prophecy given by the Holy Spirit is judged within each believer who hears it by the Holy Spirit. (1 Cor. 14:32.)

Jeremiah, who endured many afflictions, still praised God for His faithfulness. God will never give a prophecy of defeat—for God is not a God of defeat but of victory!

Faithfulness— Distinguishing Between Spirits

The Holy Spirit, as our faithful Friend and Counselor, produces the fruit of faithfulness in us. This faithfulness is after the nature of God's faithfulness, which forever is steadfast, unshakable, unmovable, and unchanging. Because God is faithful, His love is always certain. When we are faithful, our love, like His, will be constant and unwavering.

God can always trust faithful believers to be true to Him and His Word; and others should always be able to count on Christians to remain faithful in whatever circumstance or situation they find themselves. Believers who walk in faithfulness will always be reliable and trustworthy in both word and deed.

The fruit of faithfulness aids the Christian in distinguishing between spirits. Faithfulness comes through reading the Bible daily; maintaining a good prayer life; and being faithful in our churches, marriages, friendships, and businesses. When you are faithful, you are like Jesus: "The one who calls you is faithful" (1 Thess. 5:24).

There are four things a Christian can discern: (1) the Holy Spirit (John 1:32-34); (2) good angels (Acts 12:1-11); (3) evil spirits (Acts 16:16-18); and human spirits (Luke 9:53-55).

Hebrews 5:14 tells us how to distinguish between spirits-through training: "But solid food is for the mature, who by constant use have trained themselves to distinguish good from evil."

Training is an essential factor in a Christian's life, because training your spirit and senses to discern good from evil not only helps you, but it enables you to minister to others; it also protects you from false doctrine. This gift often comes through visions (Rev. 16:13,14) and dreams (Matt. 1:20,21).

Faithfulness comes through reading the Bible daily; maintaining a good prayer life; and being faithful in our churches, marriages, friendships, and businesses.

When you have matured and can discern good from evil, the Holy Spirit can use you to distinguish between spirits. This gift may be used to (1) help in delivering the afflicted and those who are oppressed of an evil spirit (Acts 16:16-18); (2) help you know a servant of the devil (Acts 13:9-11); (3) know ahead of time about a master plot of the devil so his work can be bound (Matt. 18:18-20); (4) expose error (John 16:16; 1 Tim. 4:12; 2 Peter 2:1); and (5) unmask demon miracle-workers who don't exalt the name of Jesus (1 Cor. 12:3; 1 John 4:1-3).

With all the evil in the world, it's easy to see why the fruit of faithfulness is essential for the operation of the gift of distinguishing spirits. Faithfulness is an absolute necessity in casting out demons. You can cast out the demon one day only to have it bring seven other spirits back with it to attack the person. If you're not faithful and remain with them until the whole ordeal is over, they will be in trouble.

An old expression says, "Practice makes perfect." It takes a lot of practice to be trained to distinguish between good and evil; faithfulness is essential during training. But being trained isn't enough; you must also be an eater of the Word. Notice that Jesus cast out unclean spirits by *His Word* instead of laying hands on them. (Mark 1:27.) We are told to lay hands only on the sick. (Mark 16:18.)

Gentleness—Tongues
Self-control—Interpretation of Tongues

I have combined these last two gifts because they often occur together. The Holy Spirit is always a gentleman, and the fruit He produces in God's children is always considerate, compassionate, tender, and appealing. The gentleness of the Holy Spirit is never crude or obscene. A gentle spirit is not subject to outbursts of temper or acts of selfishness. A gentle person is one who is self-controlled. Gentleness is consideration of others' feelings or circumstances, and it will attempt to heal others' hurts rather than expose them. A gentle spirit is attractive to others, and is a genteel witness of the Holy Spirit who lives in us.

If a message in tongues is given gently, it draws attention to the message and not the messenger. When Moses delivered God's message to the Pharaoh, he did it gently and exercised a lot of self-control.

The fruit of self-control is so appropriate in the life of a Spirit-filled believer. The power of the Holy Spirit's control on our lives keeps us living in the Spirit instead of living in the flesh and producing its sinful fruit. Believers who control their minds, emotions, and attitudes according to the Spirit, demonstrate temperance and godly maturity in their speech and in their actions.

Every Spirit-filled believer can use these vocal gifts of the Spirit—tongues and interpretation of tongues. You need to know that there are two kinds of tongues. Devotional tongues are for every Christian's private ministry of prayer and intercession. (1 Cor. 14:2-5.) Diverse tongues are for public ministry and must be accompanied by the gift of interpretation of tongues to avoid confusion when they are used in the church. (1 Cor.14:5-40.)

The power of the Holy Spirit's control on our lives keeps us living in the Spirit instead of living in the flesh and producing its sinful fruit.

Whenever anyone in a congregation uses the gift of tongues, the fruit of gentleness should accompany it. The message should not be given as if it were uncontrollable; rather it should be directed so believers will be edified.

A Spirit-filled Christian who prays in the Spirit strengthens his reborn spirit. That's why it's so important for every believer to have devotional tongues and exercise them: ". . . the Spirit helps us in our weakness. We do not know what we ought to pray for, but the Spirit himself intercedes for us with groans that words cannot express. And he who searches our hearts knows the mind of the Spirit, because the Spirit intercedes for the saints in accordance with God's will" (Rom. 8:26,27 NIV).

The interpretation of tongues goes along with self-control. Self-control knows when to quit. Paul said that anyone who speaks in a tongue should pray that he may interpret what he says. (1 Cor. 14:13.) The reason for this is to edify believers and convict unbelievers: "You may be giving thanks well enough, but the other man is not edified" (1 Cor. 14:17).

Harvesting the Fruit

The fruit of the Spirit in your life is meant to bring a harvest full of results. Jesus intended for us to bring forth a harvest when He said: "You did not choose me, but I chose you and appointed you to go and bear fruit–fruit that will last" (John 15:16 NIV).

The nine fruits of the Spirit can be broken into three categories representing three harvests. The first of these harvests include love, joy, and peace. They are usually seen and experienced shortly after a born-again experience, for it is at this point that you benefit the most from them.

The second harvest includes patience, kindness, and goodness; they are given so you can help others. God wants to produce a harvest *in you* and *around you*. You have the potential to be patient, kind, and good toward others, because you obtained these fruits yourself when you received Jesus. As you confess, speak, and act upon what you have already obtained, you will see the fruit of this second harvest become as big as the fruit of love, joy, and peace of the first harvest.

The third harvest consists of the last three fruit: faithfulness, gentleness, and self-control. These enable you to please God and to be a successful Christian. What is it that pleases God the most? Faith: "Without faith it is impossible to please God, because anyone who comes to him must believe that he exists and that he rewards those who earnestly seek him" (Heb. 11:6 NIV).

But faith by itself is not enough. After you have learned to walk in faith, obeying the Word even when you don't feel like it, God wants you to practice gentleness and self-control. People who are well disciplined in their spiritual walks are successful Christians, and that pleases God.

Chapter 4

Symbols of the Glory To Come

*I*n the Old Testament God gives us glimpses of the Comforter—the Helper to come. The Holy Spirit's presence runs throughout the Old Testament as a thread, leading up to the mighty Day of Pentecost, during which He was poured out on believers, infilling them with His presence.

We will find many references of how He *moves on* people, or comes upon them—but only for occasions. He did not abide *in* them. I want you to remember this in order to emphasize to you the anointing and power of the Holy Spirit you have within you in this day.

King David is an excellent example of how the Holy Spirit dwelled upon him. When King David sinned miserably by committing adultery, he prayed, "Cast me not away from thy presence; and take not thy Holy Spirit from me" (Ps. 51:11). David was saying he couldn't do without God's presence, which had rested with him before he sinned.

The Holy Spirit did not lead and guide Old Testament believers as He does today. Before the Holy Spirit was poured out on believers to indwell, or live in them, they had other avenues in which the Holy Spirit helped them discern God's guidance. In the book of Acts, before the Day of Pentecost, we find a need for selection of Judas's replacement. The disciples chose a man named Matthias by casting lots.

Remember that the disciples hadn't received the indwelling of the Holy Spirit yet, so they had to rely on the God-ordained method of casting lots. In the Old Testament, the high priests had something called the *Urim* and *Thummim*, which they cast into their laps in order to get a yes or no answer concerning God's will on any given situation. *Urim* and *Thummim* mean "lights and perfection."[1]

After the Day of Pentecost, believers can now know God's light and His perfect will for every situation through the Holy Spirit within them.

The Gospels tell us that even Jesus did no mighty works until He was baptized in the Holy Spirit. After that, He had the Spirit without measure.

Before we launch into the great, Holy Spirit-inspired exploits of the Old Testament heroes of faith, let's look at the Bible's first mention of the Holy Spirit. Everything the Holy Spirit is in the Old Testament, and everything He is in the New Testament, He is to you. So whatever He does in and through the lives of the individuals we will examine, He will do in you. He is not a respecter of persons, so all the things the Old Testament shows us we can expect—and more.

I began reading through my Bible to see in particular the Holy Spirit. I found that He is mentioned eighty-eight times, manifesting Himself in varied and unique ways. Genesis 1:2, the first reference to Him, tells us the Holy Spirit moved in creation:

And the earth was without form, and void; and darkness was upon the face of the deep. And the Spirit of God moved upon the face of the water.

Notice that everything was without form—empty, void, and dark—but when the Spirit came, He brought life.

Sometimes you may feel empty and void or that you're in darkness. As in creation, the presence of the Holy Spirit can come and fill the void in your life, and give you direction and bring life and light to your darkness.

> **The presence of the Holy Spirit can come and fill the void in your life and give you direction and bring life and light to your darkness.**

In Genesis we see that the Holy Spirit moved on people. Remember that He's called to you and me to move people and things in order to help us succeed in every area of life.

In the book of Judges, we see that the Spirit came upon Gideon to help him. (Jud. 6:34.) The angel of the Lord appeared to Gideon and proclaimed, "The Lord is with thee, thou mighty man of valour" (Jud. 6:12).

Dumbfounded, Gideon stammered, "Who, *me?* But I'm not even smart! My family's poor, and we live on the wrong side of the tracks. You can't mean me!"

But the angel of the Lord knew Gideon would be clothed with the Spirit, who would *transform* him.

Indeed, after the Spirit came upon Gideon, he delivered the Israelites out of the hands of their enemies with only three hundred men—and they faced an army of seventy-two thousand Midianites! He went on to become a great ruler over Israel because the Holy Spirit came upon him, transformed him, and worked miracles through him.

Pictures of Things To Come

The Bible is a picture book, and the Old Testament gives us "pictures," foreshadowing things to come. Throughout the Bible, God reveals the One called alongside to help. Many of the references to the Spirit in the Old Testament are symbolic of what was to come. In Ezekiel, the prophet saw a vision of "dead bones," which God breathed upon with the wind of His Spirit:

> **Come from the four winds, O breath, and breathe upon these slain, that they may live.**
>
> **Ezekiel 37:9**

That breath of God brought life, just as the Holy Spirit brings life to you in the new covenant.

The New Testament also speaks of the Holy Spirit as the breath of God. After His resurrection, Jesus wanted to emphasize the Holy Spirit to His disciples; the Bible says, "He breathed on them, and saith unto them, Receive ye the Holy Ghost" (John 20:22).

The Holy Spirit is referred to again as wind in John 3:5-8, and although this story is a part of the New Testament, the people were still living under the old covenant. Jesus describes the new birth to a man named Nicodemus:

Except a man be born of water and of the Spirit, he cannot enter into the kingdom of God. That which is born of the flesh is flesh; and that which is born of the Spirit is spirit. Marvel not that I said unto thee, Ye must be born again.

The wind bloweth where it listeth, and thou hearest the sound thereof, but canst not tell whence it cometh, and whither it goeth: so is every one that is born of the Spirit.

Nicodemus has a difficult time grasping this and says, "What— do I have to enter my mother's womb again? I can't do that!" What Jesus meant was that the Spirit of God begins to move in our lives and "blow" on us as He wills.

When I was younger, the wind of the Holy Spirit began blowing on me once I was born again. At first I didn't sense Him. It wasn't some big gale; He didn't blow me down. He just blew gently, giving me a hunger to pray and read the Bible and bringing the right people into my life.

One night I was standing in a meeting and praising the Lord, and I had an unusual encounter with the Holy Spirit. I began to rock back and forth almost involuntarily. It was gentle and sweet. Ordinarily I'm quite conservative, so I thought, *God, what is this? This is strange to me!*

God answered, *That's the Holy Spirit, and I want to show you that I blow you where I want you to go. Just stay sweet in Me.*

The Holy Spirit can come into your life like a sweet, gentle breeze. Then again, sometimes the Spirit comes like a rushing mighty gale as we read about in Acts 2:2, when the disciples were all filled with the Holy Spirit.

Water is another picture of the Holy Spirit in the Bible. When you were born again, you were given a spring on the inside of you, and that spring is the Holy Spirit. Sometimes you may need a long refreshing drink. At other times, He can be the water that flows out of you to others to wash and refresh them. In Psalm 72:6 He comes down like rain. Perhaps you have gone to church on occasion feeling dry, and the Holy Spirit rained on you. He can be a well. He can be rain. He can be a river.

Hosea 14:5 speaks of the Holy Spirit coming like the morning dew. I love getting up and praying early in the morning. In the early morning I see the dew, while the world is quiet; after the sun rises, the sounds of life begin, and the sun melts the dew. I have found that when I rise early to pray, the Holy Spirit comes quietly, gently, and oh so sweetly to me, like the dew.

Fire is yet another way the Holy Spirit revealed Himself in the Bible. Each time Moses went to commune with God on Mount Sinai, he entered the presence of God's glory through a cloud. To the natural eyes, however, God's glory appeared as a consuming fire:

Mount Sinai was covered with smoke, because the Lord descended on it in fire. The smoke billowed up from it like smoke from a furnace, the whole mountain trembled violently, and the sound of the trumpet grew louder and louder. Then Moses spoke and the voice of God answered him.

To the Israelites the glory of the Lord looked like a consuming fire on top of the mountain. Then Moses

entered the cloud as he went on up the mountain. And he stayed on the mountain forty days and forty nights

Exodus 19:18,19; 24:17,18 NIV

Unlike fire in the natural realm, the fire of the Holy Spirit cannot be contained. As a "pillar" of fire, He illuminated the path of the Israelites and protected them; but as a "consuming" fire, He proclaimed God's sovereignty, wrath, and omnipotence. The Israelites feared this display of the Holy Spirit because they didn't "know" God the Father, God the Son, or God the Holy Spirit.

The *King James Version* of Psalm 103:7 says, "He made known his *ways* unto Moses, his *acts* unto the children of Israel." As born-again believers, we have a personal relationship with God, through His Son, Jesus Christ; and the fire of the Holy Spirit indwells us. Unlike the Israelites, we can know God on an intimate basis and can hear directly from the throne room through the Holy Spirit. As He indwells us, His fire utterly consumes us, burning off the chaff, weights, and sins that could hinder the plan and purpose God has for us.

When Moses dedicated the first tabernacle housing God's glory, he carefully arranged all the furniture according to God's instructions. Then a cloud of God's glory enveloped it. The Bible says, "For the cloud of the Lord was upon the tabernacle by day, and fire was on it by night" (Ex. 40:38).

The prophet Elijah encountered the fire of the Holy Spirit as well. He confronted prophets of Baal, a pagan idol. (1 Kings 18:21-28.) Elijah and the

As He indwells us, His fire utterly consumes us, burning off the chaff, weights, and sins that could hinder the plan and purpose God has for us.

prophets agreed to call upon their gods. The god who answered by sending fire to consume the sacrifice they had prepared would be the true, living God.

Of course, the prophets of Baal called upon their gods from morning till evening to no avail. Then Elijah began to pray—after soaking the sacrifice with water *three times.* After he had called upon the Lord, the Bible says, "Then the fire of the Lord fell, and consumed the burnt sacrifice" (v. 38).

Twice in the Old Testament fire came down upon the sacrifice. The temple signified the presence of God. At the dedication of the temple, the Holy Spirit came down upon it with fire and filled it with His presence.

Then, in the New Testament, John the Baptist speaks of Jesus' baptizing "with the Holy Ghost, and with fire" (Matt. 3:11). The fire falls on a new temple. What's the new temple? *We are!*

First Corinthians 6:19 says;

> **Know ye not that your body is the temple of the Holy Ghost which is in you, which ye have of God, and ye are not your own?**

In the New Testament, born-again believers now house the presence of God, and when we are baptized in the Holy Spirit, He falls upon us with His fire and consumes the sacrifice of our "temples"—our bodies. (Rom. 12:1.)

The word *temple* there is talking about the Holy of Holies. The Old Testament temple is comprised of the outer court, the Holy Place, and the Holy of Holies, but the Scripture in 1 Corinthians uses the word *naos,* which means "temple."[2] You are a temple, and your spirit is the Holy of Holies. You've got a soul—that's the Holy Place, and you've got a body—that's the outer court.

God doesn't meet you in the outer court nor in the Holy Place. He meets you in the Holy of Holies; the sacred place where His Spirit dwells.

The Symbol of Pentecost

In the Old Testament, Pentecost is the birth of the Jewish nation—the day God gave Moses the Law, the Ten Commandments they were to live by. (Ex. 20.)

Fifteen hundred years later, God sent another Pentecost—this time the birth of the Church. The two provide quite a comparison and contrast.

First, let's get some background on the Old Testament Pentecost. For fifteen hundred years, every fiftieth day following the offering of the barley sheaf at the Feast of Unleavened Bread (part of the larger celebration of Passover), the Israelites celebrated the Feast of Weeks or the Feast of Harvest (called *Pentecost*—Greek for "fifty"[3]).

> **God doesn't meet you in the outer court. He meets you in the Holy of Holies; the sacred place where His Spirit dwells.**

The Jews trace their first Pentecost back to the giving of the Law on Mt. Sinai, the birthplace and birthday of Judaism. The New Testament Pentecost was the birthday of Christianity. Paul compares and contrasts these two Pentecosts in 2 Corinthians 3.

Old Testament Pentecost

- The fiftieth day
- Writing of Ten Commandments on two tables of stone

- Commandments written by the finger of God
- Three thousand people slain
- A ministration of death
- The letter
- Glory on the face of Moses
- Face veiled so people could not behold the glory
- Glory to be done away
- Ministers of old covenant
- Mt. Sinai

New Testament Pentecost
- The fiftieth day
- Writing of commandments of love on tables of the heart and mind
- Commandments written by the Spirit of God
- Three thousand people live
- A ministration of life
- The Spirit
- Glory on the face of Jesus
- Unveiled face so we can be changed into the same glory
- Glory that remains
- Ministers of the new covenant
- Mt. Zion

Both Old and New Testament Pentecosts began on the fiftieth day. They were marked by fire and wind; Exodus 19:18 tells us that Mount Sinai—the mountain Moses ascended to meet God—began to quake and was lit by fire and swept by wind.

> **And mount Sinai was altogether on a smoke, because the Lord descended upon it in fire: and the smoke thereof ascended as the smoke of a furnace, and the whole mount quaked greatly.**

Both the births of the old covenant and the new covenant came by fire:

> **And suddenly there came a sound from heaven as of a rushing mighty wind, and it filled all the house where they were sitting. And there appeared unto them cloven tongues like as of fire, and it sat upon each of them.**
>
> **Acts 2:2,3**

In the Old Testament, there was the writing of the Ten Commandments on two tables of stone, but God said in the New Testament that He wouldn't write His commandments, His Word, on tables of stone; He said He would write them on our hearts:

> **Ye are manifestly declared to be the epistle of Christ...written not with ink, but with the Spirit of the living God; not in tables of stone, but in fleshy tables of the heart.**
>
> **2 Corinthians 3:3**

Exodus 31:18 tells us the Ten Commandments were written with the finger of God, but in the New Testament, He writes His commandments by the Holy Spirit.

Three thousand people were killed on the Day of Pentecost when God gave the Law, but on the New Testament Day of Pentecost, three thousand were saved. The New Testament is a *better* covenant!

81

The old covenant was a ministration of death by the letter of the Law. People said, "Oh no, I'm a sinner; this Law proves it to me, but I don't know how to get out of it."

By contrast, the new covenant is a ministration of the Spirit. In it, you can say, "I don't know how to do this in my flesh, but 'The law of the Spirit of life in Christ Jesus hath made me free from the law of sin and death'" (Rom. 8:2). The Holy Spirit, your Helper, gives you power over sin through the new covenant!

Glory was present during the giving of both the old and new covenants. When God gave the old covenant, there was such glory on the face of Moses that he had to put a veil over his face. The people couldn't behold the glory of God in such splendor.

2 Corinthians 3:18 says in the new covenant:

We all, with open face beholding as in a glass the glory of the Lord, are changed into the same image from glory to glory, even as by the Spirit of the Lord.

This is what the outpouring of the Spirit on the New Testament Day of Pentecost brought. The glory remains! The glory had to be veiled on Mount Sinai, but we received our Pentecost on Mount Zion:

For ye are not come unto the mount that might be touched, and that burned with fire, nor unto blackness, and darkness, and tempest, and the sound of a trumpet, and the voice of words; which voice they that heard intreated that the word should not be spoken to them any more: (For they could not endure that which was commanded, and if so much as a beast touch the mountain, it shall be stoned, or thrust through with a dart: and

so terrible was the sight, that Moses said, I exceedingly fear and quake:)

But ye are come unto mount Sion, and unto the city of the living God, the heavenly Jerusalem, and to an innumerable company of angels, to the general assembly and church of the firstborn, which are written in heaven, and to God the Judge of all, and to the spirits of just men made perfect, and to Jesus the mediator of the new covenant.

Hebrews 12:18-24

Since the Old Testament provides us with pictures of what was to come in the New Testament, you must have the Old Testament to compare it with, or you won't get the full picture God's trying to give us in the New Testament. All these comparisons we've looked at are pointing the way to the Holy Spirit, who would be poured out on believers on the New Testament Day of Pentecost.

The Old Testament points the way to a new and better covenant, one in which the Holy Spirit abides within believers as God's new temple. No longer does He dwell upon believers; the Holy Spirit now fills and empowers believers, beginning with the "second" Pentecost and the birth of the Church.

Chapter 5

Acts of the Holy Spirit

But ye shall receive power, after that the Holy Ghost is come upon you: and ye shall be witnesses unto me both in Jerusalem, and in all Judaea, and in Samaria, and unto the uttermost part of the earth.

Acts 1:8

Do you ever want to just hang out with Jesus? When we read the book of Acts, we're looking at the book in which Jesus really "hangs out" with the believers through the person of the Holy Spirit, and this is normal—we could say it's standard operating procedure for believers. That's the way the Church began.

And the Church will not end in defeat. The Bible says that as Jesus is, so are we. Jesus Himself said, "He that believeth on me, the works that I do shall he do also" (John 14:12). The Holy Spirit is bringing the Church alive to see who we really are in Christ—and who Christ is in us. The more we understand this, the more we begin to operate in the supernatural.

The book of Acts is a study of the believers' realizing who they are in Christ and thus how they operate in the supernatural through the Holy Spirit. It is the standard operating procedure for the believer today; in other words, the things that happened in the book of Acts should be occurring in our lives today, because the same Holy Spirit in Acts dwells in us.

Let's begin our study with Jesus' ascension in Acts 1:9,10:

And when he [Jesus] had spoken these things, while they beheld, he was taken up; and a cloud received him out of their sight.

Imagine the apostles' distress as they watched the physical body of Jesus ascending out of their sight! For three-and-a-half years God had been manifested in the flesh-and-blood body of Jesus Christ. The evidence for His divinity was compelling: men raised from the dead, blind eyes opened, deaf ears unstopped, the crippled walking, lepers cleansed, five thousand fed, and even a walk on the water—all performed through the power of the Holy Spirit. Now the body in which He "began both to do and teach" (Acts 1:1) was vanishing into the clouds!

Jesus did not cease to exist; but for our sake His physical body ascended out of view to make way for the new, corporate Body in which He would continue "to do and teach." That Body is His Church—a supernatural phenomenon much like the burning bush of the Old Testament, burning yet unconsumed. (Ex. 3.) God had spoken to Moses from a burning bush, and now, fifteen hundred years later, God wanted to speak to all the world through the "burning bush" of His Church.

The purpose of the Church is to do and teach through the outpouring of the Holy Spirit. The miracles and teachings of Jesus are to continue until the end of the age when Jesus returns, and the Church is to be a burning, shining light of signs and wonders.

> **The Church is to be a burning, shining light of signs and wonders.**

On the Day of Pentecost God lit the fire. The outpouring of the Holy Spirit at Pentecost, according to Acts 1:8, was to empower those who were present in the Upper Room to be Jesus' witnesses:

> **Ye shall receive power, after that the Holy Ghost is come upon you: and ye shall be witnesses unto me both in Jerusalem, and in all Judaea, and in Samaria, and unto the uttermost part of the earth.**

According to Webster's Dictionary, *witness* means "evidence."[1] It's not just talking about Jesus; it's evidence. Although Jesus—who was the physical evidence of God's existence—was gone, the evidence nevertheless remained in the life of each person indwelled by the Holy Spirit. The witness, or evidence, to the fact of Jesus' resurrection and the Spirit's outpouring is still evident today. The world is now to behold Jesus in His many-membered Body.

The true Body of Christ will always present supernatural phenomena to the world, just as Jesus did. When Peter stood up to preach after having received the Holy Spirit, a man who had been fearful and cringing just days earlier was suddenly a prophet, apostle, and evangelist with the fire of God in his heart. Peter was certainly a witness, or evidence, that what Jesus had begun while in His physical body was continuing—in this instance through a Galilean fisherman.

We are God's burning bush— on fire, but never consumed.

The acts of the Holy Spirit through the Church continue *today* in you and me. We are God's burning bush—on fire, but never consumed. Internal and external pressures may try to smother this flame, but God's Spirit burns eternally in the hearts of men and women who have been born again. The book of Acts is the story of how this flame began, overcame every attempt to put out its light, and spread victoriously throughout all the earth.

The Author

We know from their prologues that Luke was the author of both the gospel that bears his name and the book of Acts:

> **Forasmuch as many have taken in hand to set forth in order a declaration of those things which are most surely believed among us...it seemed good to me also, having had perfect understanding of all things from the very first, to write unto thee in order, most excellent Theophilus.**
>
> **Luke 1:1,3**

> **The former treatise have I made, O Theophilus, of all that Jesus began both to do and teach.**
>
> **Acts 1:1**

In both books, Luke addresses Theophilus. In a sense, Theophilus is you and I. *Theophilus* comes from two words—*theo* and *phileo*—which means "God-loved."[2] The book of Acts is written to the God-loved, and therefore it is written to us.

"Luke, the beloved physician, and Demas, greet you" (Col. 4:14).

We first encounter Luke in the book of Acts in the story which takes place in Troas. It was there that he first began to use the term *we* in his account:

> **And after he [Paul] had seen the vision, immediately we endeavoured to go into Macedonia, assuredly gathering that the Lord had called us for to preach the gospel unto them. Therefore loosing from Troas, we came with a straight course to Samothracia, and the next day to Neapolis.**
>
> **Acts 16:10,11**

Paul's mention in Colossians 4:10-14 of three friends who were "of the circumcision" suggests that Luke was a Gentile. In fact, he may have been one of Paul's converts. As such, Luke is the only non-Jewish writer of the New Testament.

Luke stayed with Paul throughout his ministry, even through the rough times of Paul's imprisonment. Writing during his second Roman imprisonment, Paul said, "Only Luke is with me" (2 Tim. 4:11).

Luke's careful investigation, eyewitness accounts, and Holy Spirit-inspired writing give us a marvelous glimpse of the early Church—its birth, growth, trials, and triumphs.

Chapter 6

Special Delivery

(*Acts 1:3-2:4*)

*I*f you've ever been present at a birth, you know the awe and wonder at the entrance into this world of a newborn. What emotion! What joy!

Now imagine your heavenly Father's joy at the birth of the Church—something planned for by the Trinity in eternity past and looked forward to for centuries. Matthew 16:18 says, "I will build my church; and the gates of hell shall not prevail against it."

God built such a Church on the power of the Holy Spirit. Then and only then would the signs and wonders of the Church shake hell to pieces. However, the descent of the Holy Spirit to birth the Church required the ascension of the One who had prophesied the birth of the Church. The Spirit could not be sent until Jesus was glorified:

> **In the last day, that great day of the feast, Jesus stood and cried, saying, If any man thirst, let him come unto me, and drink. He that believeth on me, as the scripture hath said, out of his belly shall flow rivers of living water. (But this spake he of the Spirit, which they that believe on him should receive: for the Holy Ghost was not yet given; because that Jesus was not yet glorified.)**
>
> **John 7:37-39**

On that great Feast Day before His death and resurrection, Jesus prophesied of the outpouring of the Holy Spirit on the Day of Pentecost, a celebration coming fifty days after Passover.

Preparation for the Spirit's Indwelling

For forty days after His resurrection, Jesus came and went among His followers. He prepared them for the time when they would no longer have His physical presence in their midst. They would soon know Him in an entirely different way:

> **And I will pray the Father, and he shall give you another Comforter, that he may abide with you for ever; even the Spirit of truth; whom the world cannot receive because it seeth him not, neither knoweth him: but ye know him; for he dwelleth with you, and shall be in you. I will not leave you comfortless: I will come to you.... At that day ye shall know that I am in my Father, and ye in me, and I in you.**
>
> **John 14:16-18,20**

> **Wherefore henceforth know we no man after the flesh: yea, though we have known Christ after the flesh, yet now henceforth know we him no more.**
>
> **2 Corinthians 5:16**

This baptism of the Holy Spirit was one of the "things pertaining to the kingdom of God" that Jesus spoke about before His departure in the clouds (Acts 1:3). This was not the first time He had instructed His disciples concerning the promised Holy Spirit:

> **And, being assembled together with them, commanded them that they should not depart from Jerusalem, but wait for the promise of the Father, which, saith he, ye have heard of me.**
>
> **Acts 1:4**

John the Baptist had also foretold of this Holy Spirit baptism:

> **I indeed baptize you with water unto repentance: but he that cometh after me is mightier than I, whose shoes I am not worthy to bear: he shall baptize you with the Holy Ghost, and with fire.**
>
> **Matthew 3:11**

And again:

> **And [John] preached, saying, There cometh one mightier than I after me, the latchet of whose shoes I am not worthy to stoop down and unloose. I indeed have baptized you with water: but he shall baptize you with the Holy Ghost.**
>
> **Mark 1:7,8**

Whenever I read this first chapter of Acts, I am encouraged. Because of the disciples' question to Jesus in verse 6, I know there are never any stupid questions as far as God is concerned! Jesus had just spent forty days speaking to them about the things pertaining to the kingdom, and yet they were *still* unclear about God's program for the Jews and Gentiles:

> **When they therefore were come together, they asked of him, saying, Lord, wilt thou at this time restore again the kingdom to Israel? And he said unto them, It is not for you to know the times or the seasons, which the Father hath put in his own power.**
>
> Acts 1:6,7

Jesus was so patient with them. He didn't slap His forehead and moan, "I can't believe it! What have I been talking about these past forty days? Haven't you been listening?" No, instead He gently told them not to worry about the timing of the kingdom. He turned their attention to something of more immediate importance:

> **But ye shall receive power, after that the Holy Ghost is come upon you: and ye shall be witnesses unto me both in Jerusalem, and in all Judaea, and in Samaria, and unto the uttermost part of the earth.**
>
> Acts 1:8

The timing of the kingdom was the Father's business; the witnessing with power to the uttermost part of the earth was the disciples' business. This power was *dunamis* in the Greek language—miracle-working power.[3] We get our word *dynamite* from *dunamis*. This was the kind of power necessary to take the news throughout the earth.

These were Jesus' last recorded words while on earth. Remember, last words are usually the most important. If I'm leaving to go to the store or to visit a friend, my last words to my husband are the ones I want him to remember most: "Don't forget to turn off the stove!" or "Don't forget to let the dog out!"

The most important subject on Jesus' mind before He ascended was the miracle-working power of the Holy Spirit that He was going to send upon His disciples.

> **The most important subject on Jesus' mind before He ascended was the miracle-working power of the Holy Spirit that He was going to send upon His disciples.**

The Ascension

Having said His parting words, Jesus returned to the glory He had left some thirty-three years earlier:

And when he had spoken these things, while they beheld, he was taken up; and a cloud received him out of their sight.

Acts 1:9

Imagine the emotion experienced by those disciples who stood watching Jesus leave their sight! This One who spoke and acted like no other in the history of man was no longer going to be physically present with them. The disciples, despite the promise of the Holy Spirit, felt emptiness and a loss that, if not checked, would have overwhelmed them. Their heavenly Father graciously provided a word of encouragement and comfort to them through two angels standing nearby:

> **And while they looked steadfastly toward heaven as he went up, behold, two men stood by them in white apparel; which also said, Ye men of Galilee, why stand ye gazing up into heaven? This same Jesus, which is taken up from you into heaven, shall so come in like manner as ye have seen him go into heaven.**
>
> Acts 1:10,11

A Replacement for Judas

Following the Ascension, the disciples returned to the Upper Room in Jerusalem. This was in obedience to the Lord's command:

> **And, being assembled together with them, [Jesus] commanded them that they should not depart from Jerusalem, but wait for the promise of the Father, which, saith he, ye have heard of me.**
>
> Acts 1:4

Obedience always results in blessing! The Holy Spirit wasn't going to be sent to Rome, to Samaria, or to any location outside of Jerusalem. Anyone who chose to ignore the Lord's words, to spiritualize them away, would miss out on the initial outpouring of the promised Comforter and *dunamis* power that would turn the world upside down.

Evidently the eleven disciples took up temporary residence in the Upper Room; verse 13 tells us they "abode" there at this time. Jesus had told them to wait for the promise of the Father. This waiting lasted about ten days and was a time of prayer:

These all continued with one accord in prayer and supplication, with the women, and Mary the mother of Jesus, and with his brethren.

Acts 1:14

The Greek word for *continued* means "persevered."[4] They persevered with one purpose in prayer. Don't you know that those believers were precious to the Lord? They were the small handful of *seed* that God was going to use to *sow* the gospel into all the world. The *harvest* would stretch over two thousand years and include you and me!

> The reason we don't see more of the outpouring of the Holy Spirit is that we don't always come together in one accord.

Notice also that verse says they were all *in one accord.* The reason we don't see more of the outpouring of the Holy Spirit is that we don't always come together in one accord. We're unhappy about this or that, upset with someone or another. We are empowered through the Holy Spirit to be like Jesus. Jesus is not upset with anybody!

Many times churches lack the power of the Holy Spirit because they are in discord rather than one accord; so we have to remember to come to the Father as this verse instructs us: in one accord.

Now, those waiting in the Upper Room included Jesus' mother and *brethren.* The Greek word used here means "of the same womb."[5] These "rethren were literally half-brothers to Jesus. These were the same brethren who earlier had not believed that Jesus was the Messiah: "For neither did his brethren believe in him" (John 7:5).

Obviously His family did a turnaround! They all persevered in the Upper Room, waiting to receive the baptism of the Holy Spirit.

Chapter 7

Power From Another Helper

(Acts 2:5-4:31)

After you gain an understanding of the Old Testament, it plays an important factor in understanding the New Testament. For example, Acts 2:5 tells us that there were Jews from "every nation under heaven" living (and no doubt visiting) in Jerusalem around the Day of Pentecost. Why would these Jews be out of every nation under heaven? Why hadn't they lived in Israel all their lives? What brought them to Jerusalem at this time of year?

For the answers, we have to go back to the books of Exodus and Leviticus. When God delivered the Israelites out of Egypt, He commanded them to keep three national holidays, or feasts:

> **Three times thou shalt keep a feast unto me in the year. Thou shalt keep the feast of unleavened bread** [Passover]...**and the feast of harvest** [Pentecost], **the first-fruits of thy labours, which thou hast sown in the field: and the feast of ingathering** [Tabernacles], **which is in the end of the year, when thou hast gathered in thy labours out of the field.**
>
> Exodus 23:14-16

The Jews couldn't celebrate these holidays just anywhere; God chose Jerusalem as the site for the feasts:

> **Three times in a year shall all thy males appear before the Lord thy God in the place which he shall choose.**
>
> Deuteronomy 16:16

Pentecost was the celebration of harvest time; the waving of two loaves of bread marked it by the priest:

> **And ye shall count unto you from the morrow after the sabbath, from the day that ye brought the sheaf of the wave offering; seven sabbaths shall be complete: even unto the morrow after the seventh sabbath shall ye number fifty days; and ye shall offer a new meat offering unto the Lord.**
>
> **Ye shall bring out of your habitations two wave loaves of two tenth deals: they shall be of fine flour; they shall be baken with leaven; they are the firstfruits unto the Lord.**
>
> Leviticus 23:15-17

The two loaves of bread certainly represent the two peoples—Jews and Gentiles—who compose the Lord's Body. Pentecost shows us that we are part of the end-time harvest and the end-time outpouring of God's Spirit.

Acts 2:1-4 are familiar verses to many people. Let's look at these four verses one at a time:

> **And when the day of Pentecost was fully come, they were all with one accord in one place.**
>
> **Acts 2:1**

Jesus had started with 12 disciples; now there were 120 waiting in the Upper Room. The prayer and unity of this group set the stage for the Holy Spirit's arrival, and the outpouring of the Holy Spirit was accompanied by two outward manifestations:

> **And suddenly there came a sound from heaven as of a rushing mighty wind, and it filled all the house where they were sitting. And there appeared unto them cloven tongues like as of fire, and it sat upon each of them.**
>
> **Acts 2:2,3**

Both the sense of sound and the sense of sight were involved in this event. There were actually three signs given as a witness to the Spirit's arrival: the mighty rushing wind, the cloven tongues like as of fire, and the speaking with other tongues.

The Church began with "a sound from heaven," and it will end with a sound from heaven:

> **For the Lord himself shall descend from heaven with a shout, with the voice of the archangel, and with the trump of God: and the dead in Christ shall rise first.**
>
> **1 Thessalonians 4:16**

The first sound from heaven on the Day of Pentecost brought the filling of the Holy Spirit:

> **And they were all filled with the Holy Ghost, and began to speak with other tongues, as the Spirit gave them utterance.**
>
> **Acts 2:4**

Now, the multitude of multilingual Jews had come to Jerusalem to celebrate Passover, and they stayed the fifty-day interval before Pentecost rather than go all the way home and come back. Acts 2:9-11 shows the geographical extent of this multitude:

> **Parthians, and Medes, and Elamites, and the dwellers in Mesopotamia, and in Judaea, and Cappadocia, in Pontus and Asia, Phrygia, and Pamphylia, in Egypt, and in the parts of Libya about Cyrene, and strangers of Rome, Jews and proselytes, Cretes and Arabians.**

Our God is so economical! He took this perfect opportunity to birth His Church and to spread the news of His Son's death and resurrection, and He did it through the gift of tongues given to a group of "ignorant" Galileans:

> **And they were all filled with the Holy Ghost, and began to speak with other tongues, as the Spirit gave them utterance.**
>
> **Now when this was noised abroad, the multitude came together, and were confounded, because that every man heard them speak in his own language.**
>
> **And they were all amazed and marvelled, saying one to another, Behold, are not all these which speak**

Galilaeans? And how hear we every man in our own
tongue, wherein we were born?

Acts 2:4,6-8

We know from verse 11 what was spoken in tongues:

...we do hear them speak in our tongues the
wonderful works of God.

The expression *wonderful works* can be translated "great
things," and it is used only one other time in the New Testament.[6]
Mary sang it concerning God's goodness in choosing her to be the
earthly mother of Jesus:

For he that is mighty hath done to me great things;
and holy is his name.

Luke 1:49

The disciples witnessed by the Holy Spirit the great things
about the life, death, and resurrection of the Lord Jesus. This
supernatural occurrence of speaking in tongues resulted in three
reactions: some were amazed and acknowledged God's supernatural manifestation; others doubted and questioned; still others
mocked, accusing the disciples of being drunk.

It is the same today! Some come to our meetings and say, "This
is supernatural; God is speaking to me"; others say, "I don't know
about all this speaking in tongues business." Still others openly
mock and declare, "Tongues aren't for today!"

Peter's First Sermon

Now that God had everyone's attention, He was ready to fulfill
Jesus' promise that the disciples would "receive power" once the
Holy Spirit had come upon them. Peter, the disciple who had

denied Jesus three times and gone back to fishing following the Ascension, was the first instrument God chose to use under the anointing of the newly poured out Holy Spirit:

> **But Peter, standing up with the eleven, lifted up his voice, and said unto them, Ye men of Judaea, and all ye that dwell at Jerusalem, be this known unto you, and hearken to my words.**
>
> **Acts 2:14**

Notice that Peter was standing with the other eleven—including Matthias. Rather than the disciples being drunk at only nine o'clock in the morning, Peter arrests the Jewish crowd's attention by soberly referring to a prophecy in Joel 2:28-32, which was well-known to his listeners:

> **But this is that which was spoken by the prophet Joel; And it shall come to pass in the last days, saith God, I will pour out of my Spirit upon all flesh: and your sons and your daughters shall prophesy, and your young men shall see visions, and your old men shall dream dreams: and on my servants and on my handmaidens I will pour out in those days of my Spirit; and they shall prophesy.**
>
> **And I will shew wonders in heaven above, and signs in the earth beneath; blood, and fire, and vapour of smoke: the sun shall be turned into darkness, and the moon into blood, before that great and notable day of the Lord come: and it shall come to pass, that whosoever shall call on the name of the Lord shall be saved.**
>
> **Acts 2:16-21**

How could this fisherman recite from memory such a large portion from a minor prophet like Joel? Jesus had promised them that such would be the case:

And ye shall be brought before governors and kings for my sake, for a testimony against them and the Gentiles. But when they deliver you up, take no thought how or what ye shall speak: for it shall be given you in that same hour what ye shall speak. For it is not ye that speak, but the Spirit of your Father which speaketh in you.

Matthew 10:18-20

The Holy Spirit spoke through Peter. Once he had captured the crowd's attention through Joel's prophecy, Peter quickly got to the heart of his message (recorded in Acts 2:22-24):

- Jesus was a man approved of God.

- They crucified Jesus, but that was according to God's plan.

- God raised Jesus from the dead.

Peter again quoted from the Bible—this time from David's messianic psalm in Psalm 16:8-11:

For David speaketh concerning him, I foresaw the Lord always before my face, for he is on my right hand, that I should not be moved: therefore did my heart rejoice, and my tongue was glad; moreover also my flesh shall rest in hope: because thou wilt not leave my soul in hell, neither wilt thou suffer thine Holy One to see corruption. Thou hast made known to me the ways of life; thou shalt make me full of joy with thy countenance.

Acts 2:25-28

Peter used the Jewish Scriptures to build an ironclad case that Jesus is the long-awaited Messiah, David's descendant—but also David's Lord. Jesus was not just resurrected; He was exalted and given the Holy Spirit to pour out upon all flesh, as they had just witnessed:

> **Therefore being by the right hand of God exalted, and having received of the Father the promise of the Holy Ghost, he hath shed forth this, which ye now see and hear.**
>
> **Acts 2:33**

Hallelujah! Jesus' resurrection and exaltation guarantees your resurrection!

The Church's First Altar Call

Peter's Spirit-filled words produced just the results that Jesus had predicted:

> **And when he** [the Holy Spirit] **is come, he will reprove the world of sin, and of righteousness, and of judgment: of sin, because they believe not on me; of righteousness, because I go to my Father, and ye see me no more; of judgment, because the prince of this world is judged.**
>
> **John 16:8-11**

The multitude that stood before Peter was the same multitude who had cried of Jesus, "Crucify Him! Crucify Him," fifty days earlier. Now their actions must have flashed through their minds and brought with them a sense of sin and judgment. Guilt and remorse caused them to ask the most important question anyone can ask:

Now when they heard this, they were pricked in their heart, and said unto Peter and to the rest of the apostles, Men and brethren, what shall we do?

Acts 2:37

Peter's answer to those sinners is the same answer for sinners today who want to be made right with God:

Repent, and be baptized every one of you in the name of Jesus Christ for the remission of sins, and ye shall receive the gift of the Holy Ghost.

Acts 2:38

Many among this crowd had heard John the Baptist preaching in the wilderness and baptizing those who wished to prepare their hearts for God's promised Messiah. This time the baptism would be in the name of Jesus; it would be a public acknowledgement that Jesus of Nazareth was both Messiah and Lord. Peter's preaching was anointed:

Then they that gladly received his word were baptized: and the same day there were added unto them about three thousand souls.

Acts 2:41

Isn't it just like God to reverse the curse that awaited those who had crucified His Son! Jesus had prayed, "Father, forgive them." And Peter's sermon had been the vehicle used to bring forgiveness to the very ones who deserved eternal damnation. There is always an offer of mercy from God before a pronouncement of judgment. The Lord was calling true, spiritual Israel out of the physical Israel before the final cycle of discipline mentioned in Leviticus 26 put an end to the dead, religious hypocrisy of Judaism that had turned its back on Israel's Savior. It was forty years before Jerusalem and

Isn't it just like God to reverse the curse that awaited those who had crucified His Son!

its temple were burned to the ground and leveled by Roman soldiers in 70 A.D., but by then, God's true Temple was the hearts of men and women who were filled with His Holy Spirit.

God first reached out to the Jews with the message of salvation, and the believing remnant became charter members in the Church of Jesus Christ. According to Acts 2:42, four things marked this new group of people:

1. They continued steadfastly in the apostles' doctrine.

2. They continued steadfastly in...fellowship.

3. They continued steadfastly in...breaking of bread.

4. They continued steadfastly in...prayers.

Anytime you have a group of Spirit-filled people who will give themselves to the teaching of the Word, fellowship, communion, and prayer, they will have a noticeable effect upon those around them:

And fear came upon every soul: and many wonders and signs were done by the apostles.

Acts 2:43

Communism or Christianity?

The Bible does not teach communism. Acts 2:44-45 says:

And all that believed were together, and had all things common; and sold their possessions and goods, and parted them to all men, as every man had need.

If believers are to have "all things common," it must be a work of the Holy Spirit—not the state. Nowhere in the New Testament are believers *commanded* to duplicate the Spirit's work during this special time of the Church's history. Remember that many of these new converts were from out of town; there was a genuine need for a sharing of food and lodging.

These first believers were Jews; consequently, they met daily in the temple area. What a time of joy and gladness—God was doing a new thing! Their oneness, singleness of heart, and spontaneous worship resulted in "favour with all the people" (Acts 2:47). They had great miracles, great love, great unity, great joy, and great *growth:* "And the Lord added to the church daily such as should be saved" (Acts 2:47).

If you and I will practice these same things daily—unity in the Church, singleness of heart, and worship—we will see the same results!

The Church's First Miracle of Healing

The acts of the Holy Spirit through the apostles, as we shall see, were miracles that set the stage for the preaching of the gospel. Acts 3 is devoted to the first healing miracle performed by the Holy Spirit.

It was the ninth hour, or three o'clock in the afternoon; Peter and John were still following the Jewish practice of praying toward or at the temple three times a day.

From the time they were little boys, Peter and John must have gone to the temple thousands of times to pray, but this time would be different! This time they were filled with the Holy Spirit and empowered to continue the miracle-working ministry of Jesus, and now they had another Helper working as the gifts of the Spirit worked through them.

The story is a familiar one to many: a man born handicapped begged them for alms; and although poor in material wealth, Peter was rich in spiritual power:

> **Then Peter said, Silver and gold have I none; but such as I have give I thee: In the name of Jesus Christ of Nazareth rise up and walk. And he took him by the right hand, and lifted him up: and immediately his feet and ankle bones received strength.**
>
> **Acts 3:6,7**

This first miracle of healing in the Church did more than just heal a handicapped man. All of Jerusalem must have passed this man at one time or another, and now the news of his miraculous healing spread quickly throughout the town. God was again drawing the net and preparing the way for another gospel message from Peter with the help of the Holy Spirit:

> **And as the lame man which was healed held Peter and John, all the people ran together unto them in the porch that is called Solomon's, greatly wondering. And when Peter saw it, he answered unto the people, Ye men of Israel, why marvel ye at this? or why look ye so earnestly on us, as though by our own power or holiness we had made this man to walk?**
>
> **Acts 3:11,12**

Peter's message came as the result of the miracle. Let's look at the points of his second sermon in Acts 3:12-26:

1. God has glorified Jesus through this miracle. (vv. 12,13.)

2. You killed God's Son, but God raised Him from the dead. (vv. 14,15.)

3. Faith in Jesus' name healed the lame man. (v. 16.)

4. Your actions were the result of ignorance; nevertheless, they were the fulfillment of prophecy. (vv. 17,18.)

5. Repent and you will receive forgiveness. (v. 19.)

6. Jesus will return after God has restored all things spoken by the prophets. (vv. 20,21.)

7. Moses and all the prophets spoke of Jesus and of these days. (vv. 22-25)

8. God sent Jesus to the Jews first to bless them with His forgiveness. (v. 26.)

The Church's First Persecution

There are always two responses to the gospel: people receive it or reject it. Peter and John experienced both reactions; the Sadducees rejected the message because they were "grieved" that Peter and John "preached through Jesus the resurrection from the dead" (Acts 4:2). We know why that would be upsetting to them:

For the Sadducees say that there is no resurrection, neither angel, nor spirit.

Acts 23:8

Peter's message ran contrary to the religious beliefs of these Jewish leaders. Unwilling to change their beliefs, they chose to attempt to stop to the message:

And they laid hands on them [Peter and John], **and put them in hold unto the next day: for it was now eventide.**

Acts 4:3

But the Holy Spirit through Luke is also quick to point out the other response to Peter's message:

Howbeit many of them which heard the word believed;
and the number of the men was about five thousand.

Acts 4:4

Trial and Defense: Peter's Third Sermon

The Jewish leaders couldn't argue about the miracle. Too many people had seen the handicapped man at the gate, and now he was up and walking! Instead of denying the healing took place, they wanted to accuse Peter and John of using demonic powers:

And when they had set them in the midst, they asked,
By what power, or by what name, have ye done this?

Acts 4:7

What a loaded question! It was just what Peter (and the Holy Spirit in Peter) needed to launch into another gospel sermon! This time the message is short but powerful and highly anointed:

If we this day be examined of the good deed done to the impotent man, by what means he is made whole; be it known unto you all, and to all the people of Israel, that by the name of Jesus Christ of Nazareth, whom ye cruci-fied, whom God raised from the dead, even by him doth this man stand here before you whole.

This is the stone which was set at nought of you builders, which is become the head of the corner. Neither is there salvation in any other: for there is none other

name under heaven given among men, whereby we must be saved.

Acts 4:9-12

What boldness through the Holy Spirit!

Can you believe that this is the same Peter speaking who sheepishly denied Jesus when asked about Him by a young woman? What boldness through the Holy Spirit! Peter capitalized upon their knowledge of the Scriptures to prick their hearts. He referred to Jesus as the stone rejected by them:

> **And he shall be for a sanctuary; but for a stone of stumbling and for a rock of offence to both the houses of Israel, for a gin and for a snare to the inhabitants of Jerusalem.**
>
> **Isaiah 8:14**

Jesus had earlier referred to Himself as the stone:

> **And have ye not read this scripture; The stone which the builders rejected is become the head of the corner.**
>
> **Mark 12:10**

Peter leaves them hopeless with his last statement:

> **Neither is there salvation in any other: for there is none other name under heaven given among men, whereby we must be saved.**
>
> **Acts 4:12**

"Sorry, fellows," Peter says, "you've rejected your only hope of salvation. It's decision time for you! The fact that this lame man was made whole by the name and authority of Jesus proves that God raised Jesus from the dead and that God has put His stamp of approval upon Jesus' life and message."

The Jewish elders made their decision: they rejected Peter's sermon and tried to stop the burning bush of the Spirit-filled Church that threatened to burn out of control if not stopped.

> **And they called them, and commanded them not to speak at all nor teach in the name of Jesus.**
>
> Acts 4:18

These two fishermen were not intimidated at all by the Jewish leaders. They simply responded, "Whether it be right in the sight of God to hearken unto you more than unto God, judge ye" (v. 19). Although their attitude was submissive to their leaders, they were obedient to their ultimate leader—God.

When the disciples were released, they went back to the growing group of believers and reported all that had been said and done, prayed for continued boldness and miracles, and received an immediate answer:

> **And when they had prayed, the place was shaken where they were assembled together; and they were all filled with the Holy Ghost, and they spake the word of God with boldness.**
>
> Acts 4:31

Notice the effect of persecution upon God's Church. Rather than *restrict* the saints, it *released* the saints to speak the Word with boldness. Satan's outward attempt to douse the burning bush—the Church—had failed. He didn't stop there. If outward persecution wouldn't work, there was always the possibility of corrupting the Church from within, but God's Church, as we shall see, met this challenge in the power of the Holy Spirit and grew all the stronger because of it!

Chapter 8

Prison, Praise, and Persecution

(*Acts 4:32-8:1*)

The threats of the Jewish leaders failed to have any effect upon the growing Church. Intimidation is a powerless weapon against the genuine work of the Holy Spirit within a believer's heart. I remember reading the account of a group of Christians meeting in a communist country. Their time of fellowship was interrupted by soldiers who broke up the meeting as they announced, "Anyone who wishes to renounce Jesus may leave; all others will be shot in five minutes!"

Intimidation is a powerless weapon against the genuine work of the Holy Spirit within a believer's heart.

A few people did leave the building. After it was obvious that the others would not deny the name of Jesus, the guards locked the doors and said, "We are believers in Jesus, too, but we did not want to worship with anyone who was not totally committed to Christ. May we join your group?"

Hallelujah! The presence of the Holy Spirit in a believer's life will result in boldness in the face of even death itself!

The first-century believers were living in the presence of the Holy Spirit as evidenced by two things:

1. Their actions:

> **And the multitude of them that believed were of one heart and of one soul: neither said any of them that ought of the things which he possessed was his own; but they had all things common.**
>
> **Acts 4:32**

2. Their words:

> **And with great power gave the apostles witness of the resurrection of the Lord Jesus: and great grace was upon them all.**
>
> **Acts 4:33**

Luke records the *power* of the Church:

> **And by the hands of the apostles were many signs and wonders wrought among the people...insomuch that they brought forth the sick into the streets, and laid**

them on beds and couches, that at the least the shadow of Peter passing by might overshadow some of them.

There came also a multitude out of the cities round about unto Jerusalem, bringing sick folks, and them which were vexed with unclean spirits: and they were healed every one.

Acts 5:12,15,16

Here we read a description of the Church continuing the works, which Jesus began to do. (Acts 1:1.) Luke used similar words to describe the ministry of Jesus:

And he [Jesus] came down with them, and stood in the plain, and the company of his disciples, and a great multitude of people out of all Judaea and Jerusalem, and from the sea coast of Tyre and Sidon, which came to hear him, and to be healed of their diseases; and they that were vexed with unclean spirits: and they were healed. And the whole multitude sought to touch him: for there went virtue out of him, and healed them all.

Luke 6:17-19

The healings mentioned in Luke 6 were only the beginning of what Jesus came to do; now He was continuing those works through His Body through the ministry of the Holy Spirit.

Now the Church was performing the same works through the Holy Spirit as a sign to validate the gospel message of Jesus' life, death, and resurrection. Later the apostle Paul would write, "For the Jews require a sign" (1 Cor. 1:22). God gave them "signs and wonders" to turn their hearts toward the forgiveness and new life He offered to all. Multitudes saw the signs and believed the message but not everyone believed. Whenever there are great miracles, there seems to be great persecution.

Whenever there are great miracles, there seems to be great persecution.

Despite greater persecution, the Church continued to grow. Internal or external pressures did not deter the apostles. Rather, "They ceased not to teach and preach Jesus Christ" (Acts 5:42).

Indeed, they *were* endued with power by the infilling of the Holy Spirit! (Luke 24:39.) Their Helper had come as Jesus had promised.

The Church's First Martyr: Stephen

It was now the unbelievers' turn to murmur! As we already discussed, Stephen operated mightily in the gifts of the Spirit, but the great wonders and miracles the Holy Spirit performed through him brought great opposition from a number of groups:

> **Then there arose certain of the synagogue, which is called the synagogue of the Libertines, and Cyrenians, and Alexandrians, and of them of Cilicia and of Asia, disputing with Stephen.**
>
> Acts 6:9

Here we read about five groups of Jews ganging up on one Spirit-filled layman in the church. I almost feel sorry for the Jews, because the odds were definitely stacked against them!

Every Spirit-filled believer has the same odds. No matter what obstacles or persecution we face, it's no match for the power of the Holy Spirit in us to put us over!

Now, the first group persecuting Stephen was from the synagogue of the Libertines. These were either freed Jews who left Rome when Tiberius expelled all Jews from the city around 20 A.D., or perhaps they were from the city of Libertina, Africa.

No matter what obstacles or persecution we face, it's no match for the power of the Holy Spirit in us to put us over!

And they were not able to resist the wisdom and the spirit by which he spake.

Acts 6:10

When these men couldn't win their argument legally, they resorted to illegal means by putting forth some men who lied about Stephen:

Then they suborned men, which said, We have heard him speak blasphemous words against Moses, and against God.

Acts 6:11

Once again opposition to what God was doing through His Church set up the perfect situation for preaching to the Sanhedrin, the Jewish council. Notice God's goodness in sharing the message of repentance and forgiveness so many times with these religious leaders! The Holy Spirit kept moving on their hearts, trying to bring them to repentance.

Stephen's Defense

When the high priest asked Stephen, "Are these things so?" it was just the opportunity Stephen was looking for to launch into a sermon with the help of the Holy Spirit, which included a marvelous review of Israel's history, beginning with God's appearance to Abraham. Stephen really knew the Word of God! Like Stephen, you and I can know the Word of God so well that the Holy Spirit can use us when an occasion arises that requires us to speak.

Stephen presented Israel's history down to the time of Solomon's temple. "However," he concluded to these priests who were so proud of their magnificent temple, "God doesn't dwell in man-made buildings." (Acts 7:48.) He capped his argument with a quote from Isaiah:

> **Heaven is my throne, and earth is my footstool: what house will ye build me? saith the Lord: or what is the place of my rest? Hath not my hand made all these things?**
>
> **Acts 7:49,50**

If that wasn't enough to set the religious leaders back a bit, Stephen personalized his message even more by boldly accusing the Sanhedrin of rebellion and murder:

> **Ye stiffnecked and uncircumcised in heart and ears, ye do always resist the Holy Ghost: as your fathers did, so do ye. Which of the prophets have not your fathers persecuted? and they have slain them which shewed before of the coming of the Just One; of whom ye have been now the betrayers and murderers: who have received the law by the disposition of angels, and have not kept it.**
>
> **Acts 7:51-53**

How important it is to yield to the Holy Spirit's convicting power! Once again the Jews had the option of accepting or rejecting the truth; they chose to reject it:

When they heard these things, they were cut to the heart, and they gnashed on him with their teeth.

Acts 7:54

God had the most wonderful way of keeping Stephen calm, cool, and collected. He drew heaven's curtain aside and gave Stephen discernment to get a glimpse of God's glory:

But he [Stephen], being full of the Holy Ghost, looked up stedfastly into heaven, and saw the glory of God, and Jesus standing on the right hand of God. And said, Behold, I see the heavens opened, and the Son of man standing on the right hand of God.

Acts 7:55,56

Incidentally, why do you suppose Jesus was *standing* at the Father's right hand? Everywhere else in the New Testament we read that Jesus is *seated* at the right hand of God. I believe Jesus stood in anticipation of receiving the first Christian martyr.

Then they cried out with a loud voice, and stopped their ears, and ran upon him with one accord, and cast him out of the city, and stoned him.

Acts 7:57,58

Before they picked up the boulders to throw at Stephen, the Sanhedrin laid their coats at the feet of a man named Saul. Stephen's defense and composure (I don't believe he felt any pain) at his stoning had a tremendous impact upon Saul. In fact, God answered Stephen's prayer just before his death; He transformed the Christian-hater, Saul, into the giant apostle of the faith, Paul:

And they stoned Stephen, calling upon God, and saying, Lord Jesus, receive my spirit. And he kneeled

God answered Stephen's prayer just before his death; He transformed the Christian-hater, Saul, into the giant apostle of the faith.

down, and cried with a loud voice, *Lord, lay not this sin to their charge. And when he had said this, he fell asleep.*

Acts 7:59,60

Forgiveness on our part is so important if we are to see others come into the kingdom of God. Now, Satan was so enraged at Stephen's behavior that he caused the persecution to spread throughout the Church, but we shall see that when the Church was scattered through persecution, the result backfired on the devil. The burning bush of the Spirit-filled Church that glowed so brightly in Jerusalem was flung in all directions in fulfillment of Jesus' command to take the gospel to Samaria!

Chapter 9

God Gets His Man

(Acts 8:2-9:31)

The persecution that Satan thought would eliminate the Church was the very thing that God used to spread the gospel into new areas. When Saul's persecution of the believers began, so, too, began the second stage in the development of the Church.

Up until this time, the major ministry had been under the apostles in Jerusalem. Now, the action shifted over to Philip, a deacon, which shows that the Holy Spirit uses all the members—not just the apostles—to fulfill the Great Commission.

The persecution scattered the Church, but it didn't cause it to wither and die. The Church grew from Jerusalem to Judea to

Samaria to Asia and to Rome. Persecuting a church on fire with the Holy Spirit is like kicking the embers of a fire—it scatters them, but it doesn't put them out!

In the meantime, the Church's greatest persecutor, Saul, made havoc of the Church; he was like an animal seeking its prey. After his conversion, Paul confessed to putting the Christians into prison and testifying against them before their deaths:

> **Which thing I also did in Jerusalem: and many of the saints did I shut up in prison, having received authority from the chief priests; and when they were put to death, I gave my voice against them.**
>
> **Acts 26:10**

Later Paul would write that he acted out of ignorance:

> **Who was before a blasphemer, and a persecutor, and injurious: but I obtained mercy because I did it ignorantly in unbelief.**
>
> **1 Timothy 1:13**

Samaria Hears the Gospel

As a result of the persecution, Philip traveled to the region of Samaria:

> **Then Philip went down to the city of Samaria, and preached Christ unto them.**
>
> **Acts 8:5**

Samaria was a hated place by the Jews. When the people of the Northern Kingdom were taken captive to Assyria, the king of Assyria replaced them with pagans from different countries. (2

Kings 17:24,25.) When the Jews came back from the Babylonian captivity, many of them divorced their wives to marry Samaritan women. As a result, they were not allowed to worship in the temple at Jerusalem. That didn't bother them—they built their own "temple" on Mt. Gerizim and started their own form of Judaism.

Several years ago, I had the opportunity to visit what is now called the "Temple of the Samaritans," which is in Nabulus, an Arabic city. It certainly is far from being a temple; it is more like a little house-church. Thus the Jews despised the Samaritans— but God didn't. Jesus had purposely gone through Samaria, talked to a woman there, and predicted a great harvest to come out of that city:

> **Say not ye, There are yet four months, and then cometh harvest? behold, I say unto you, Lift up your eyes, and look on the fields; for they are white already to harvest.**
>
> **John 4:35**

The persecutions of the Church and Philip's trip to Samaria were both part of the fulfillment of the harvest that Jesus saw in that town. Philip "preached Christ" to the people and performed miracles. Revival hit:

> **And the people with one accord gave heed unto those things which Philip spake, hearing and seeing the miracles which he did. And there was great joy in that city.**
>
> **Acts 8:6,8**

In contrast to the power of the Holy Spirit's flowing through Philip, we read about one Simon the sorcerer. It seems that the townspeople attributed great supernatural powers to Simon, but

Simon and his tricks were no match for Philip's preaching of the kingdom of God and the name of Jesus:

> **But when they believed Philip preaching the things concerning the kingdom of God, and the name of Jesus Christ, they were baptized, both men and women.**
>
> Acts 8:12

Luke tells us that even Simon believed and was baptized; however, I do not believe he was truly regenerated. As we shall see, his motive for "believing" was purely self-centered. He simply was amazed by the miracle-working power demonstrated by Philip:

> **Then Simon himself believed also: and when he was baptized, he continued with Philip, and wondered, beholding the miracles and signs which were done.**
>
> Acts 8:13

The revival at Samaria was such that news of it reached all the way back to Jerusalem! The apostles decided to send Peter and John down to investigate. This was the same John who had previously asked Jesus to send fire down on the Samaritans:

> **His disciples James and John...said, Lord, wilt thou that we command fire to come down from heaven, and consume them, even as Elias did?**
>
> Luke 9:54

Now God would use John to bring the fire of the Holy Spirit baptism to these same people:

Who, when they were come down, prayed for them, that they might receive the Holy Ghost: then laid they their hands on them, and they received the Holy Ghost.

Acts 8:15,17

Now we see a confrontation between the two Simons—Simon the sorcerer and Simon Peter:

And when Simon saw that through laying on of the apostles' hands the Holy Ghost was given, he offered them money. But Peter said unto him, Thy money perish with thee because thou hast thought that the gift of God may be purchased with money.

Acts 8:18,20

Peter told Simon to repent, but there doesn't seem to have been any real heart-felt repentance. Simon was more concerned about the *consequences* of his actions than anything else.

On their way back to Jerusalem, Peter and John preached the gospel in many villages of the Samaritans. True conversion will work a miracle in a person's heart attitudes. Peter and John were displaying the fruit of the Holy Spirit in their lives and making their enemies be at peace with them:

> True conversion will work a miracle in a person's heart attitudes.

When a man's ways please the Lord, he maketh even his enemies to be at peace with him.

Proverbs 16:7

At this point in the book of Acts, three parts of Jesus' command in Acts 1:8 had been fulfilled: the gospel had been preached in

Jerusalem, Judea, and Samaria. The Holy Spirit was now ready to spread God's burning bush into the uttermost parts of the earth.

A Gentile Hears the Gospel

Philip had just finished preaching to the lowly, hated Samaritans. They had given attention to his message because of the miracles of healing and casting out of demons performed in their midst. Philip's next assignment from the Holy Spirit would be quite different. This time he was sent to a spiritually hungry officer of Ethiopia who needed only to hear Philip's explanation of the Word of God in order to believe the good news about Jesus:

> **And the eunuch asked Philip, and said, I pray thee of whom speaketh the prophet this? of himself, or of some other man? Then Philip opened his mouth, and began at the same scripture, and preached unto him Jesus.**
>
> **Acts 8:34,35**

The Scripture in question was a portion of Isaiah. Philip was holding his first Bible encounter and beholding Jesus in the book of Isaiah. As Christians, we need to be so sensitive to the leading of the Holy Spirit that we are able to preach Jesus from every book of the Bible. Philip's sharing resulted in the first Gentile salvation. When the eunuch asked if he could be baptized, Philip answered:

> **If thou believest with all thine heart, thou mayest. And he answered and said, I believe that Jesus Christ is the Son of God.**
>
> **Acts 8:37**

Following his conversion, the eunuch was baptized and "went on his way rejoicing" (v. 39). The gospel and baptism of the Holy Spirit bring joy wherever they go!

Saul Meets the Risen Lord

The persecution that scattered the Christians living in Jerusalem led some to seek refuge in Damascus. Saul was determined to bring them back to Jerusalem for trial:

> **And Saul, yet breathing out threatenings and slaughter against the disciples of the Lord, went unto the high priest, and desired of him letters to Damascus to the synagogues, that if he found any of this way, whether they were men or women, he might bring them bound unto Jerusalem.**
>
> **Acts 9:1,2**

But the one who tried to arrest the believers was himself arrested as he traveled the road to Damascus. "High noon" for Saul was the time for his encounter with the Lord. Paul later recounted what happened:

> **And it came to pass, that, as I made my journey, and was come nigh unto Damascus about noon, suddenly there shone from heaven a great light round about me.**
>
> **Acts 22:6**

> **At midday...I saw in the way a light from heaven, above the brightness of the sun, shining round about me and them which journeyed with me.**
>
> **Acts 26:13**

And Acts 9:4,5 tells us Paul

...fell to the earth, and heard a voice saying unto him, Said, Saul, why persecutest thou me? And he said, Who art thou, Lord? And the Lord said, I am Jesus whom thou persecutest: it is hard for thee to kick against the pricks.

Acts 9:4,5

What were the "pricks" that Saul had kicked against? Stephen's dying words stayed in Saul's memory to haunt him. The love, zeal, and courage of the Christians he had sentenced to death assuredly never left his mind. Again and again the Holy Spirit dealt with Saul through believers, but Saul had continued to resist Him.

Then Saul, "trembling and astonished said, Lord, what wilt thou have me to do?" (Acts 9:6). Saul called Him Lord, and from that time forward, Jesus would be Lord in Saul's heart, mind, soul, and will. That day the old Saul died with Christ, and the new Saul stood forth. He would exalt Jesus perhaps as no other man ever has and operate powerfully in the Spirit. Saul was blinded physically, but he saw everything clearly with his spirit. The men with him could see with the human eye, but they really saw nothing because they failed to see Jesus.

Now was the moment that Saul would enter the fold and be baptized with fire to spread the gospel to the uttermost parts of the earth. But first, God had to use an ordinary man in Saul's life.

Have you ever been to a harbor and watched the little tugboats as they guide the huge ocean liners in and out of port? Luke introduces us now to one of God's "tugboats," who was used to launch the giant apostle of the faith into his ministry. The Lord commanded Ananias, an unknown believer living in the city of Damascus, to disciple Saul—formerly the great persecutor of the Church:

And Ananias went his way, and entered into the house; and putting his hands on him said, Brother Saul, the Lord, even Jesus, that appeared unto thee in the way as thou camest, hath sent me, that thou mightest receive thy sight, and be filled with the Holy Ghost.

Acts 9:17

Notice that Saul was already a "brother" after his encounter with Jesus. The Lord, however, chose to use a faithful new convert like Ananias to impart the baptism of the Holy Spirit to Saul.

Although he had not eaten nor drunk anything for three days, Saul's first request was to be baptized. He had seen and heard of this Christian practice that meant so much to believers. Any Jew who was publicly baptized was immediately cut off from his or her family. The new Christian was officially considered dead by parents and relatives. Thus Saul lost one family but gained a much larger and eternal one.

And with his baptism in the Holy Spirit, suddenly years and years of Old Testament study would finally come alive for Saul. Through the help of the Holy Spirit, Saul gained revelation of all the prophecies concerning the coming of the Messiah—His miracles, His rejection, His death, and His resurrection. Saul lost no time in sharing his fresh revelation of Christ in the Scriptures with the Jews at Damascus:

And straightway he preached Christ in the synagogues, that he is the Son of God.... But Saul increased the more in strength, and confounded the Jews which dwelt at Damascus, proving that this is very Christ.

Acts 9:20,22

Saul's preaching was not well received by some; they took counsel to kill him! Between his escape from Damascus and his visit to Jerusalem, Saul spent three years praying and meditating before the Lord.

The Lord used another middleman, this time Barnabus, to further the work He wanted to do through Saul:

> **When Saul was come to Jerusalem, he assayed to join himself to the disciples: but they were all afraid of him, and believed not that he was a disciple. But Barnabus took him, and brought him to the apostles, and declared unto them how he had seen the Lord in the way, and that he had spoken to him, and how he had preached boldly at Damascus in the name of Jesus.**
>
> **Acts 9:26,27**

Because of another attempt on Saul's life in Jerusalem, the Christians there sent him away to his hometown of Tarsus.

We don't read much of Paul until Acts 11:30, nearly ten years later. He went to the synagogues there to confront the Jews with the good news of Jesus Christ, their Messiah. Meanwhile, the Holy Spirit was using the apostle Peter to perform miracles and to open the door of salvation to a God-fearing Gentile named Cornelius.

Chapter 10

The Gentiles Get the Message

(Acts 9:32-12:25)

*J*esus taught His disciples a great deal about the Holy Spirit, and He also told them of a time when the Spirit would come upon them and fill them with His mighty power. This was a promise from God the Father. The Holy Spirit would move believers into such a supernatural, dynamic power that they would have ability from the Spirit to do the same kind of miraculous work Jesus did:

> I [Jesus] **tell you the truth, anyone who has faith in me will do what I have been doing. He will do even**

greater things than these, because I am going to the Father

John 14:12 NIV

Today many in the Church of Jesus Christ would try to tell us that miracles have ceased. "Miracles were for the early Church," these people argue, but don't you believe it! The Holy Spirit is still operating through believers to perform signs and wonders. As we shall see, the Lord used miracles to expand the first-century Church—which raises the question, "Does the twenty-first-century Church need to expand?" Yes! God's true Church will always operate in the supernatural in fulfilling the Great Commission of making disciples of all nations:

> **Go ye therefore, and teach all nations, baptizing them in the name of the Father, and of the Son, and of the Holy Ghost: teaching them to observe all things whatsoever I have commanded you: and, lo, I am with you always, even unto the end of the world. Amen.**

Matthew 28:19,20

The Holy Spirit, through Luke, is careful to tell us not only what happened at the hands of the apostles, but also the results of what happened.

The story of Peter's healing of a paralyzed man is a case in point. Luke tells us that Peter said, "Jesus Christ maketh thee whole: arise, and make thy bed" (Acts 9:34). The man "arose immediately." That's *what* happened; now notice the *result*:

> **And all that dwelt at Lydda and Saron saw him, and turned to the Lord.**

Acts 9:35

Hallelujah! The miracle turned a whole region around! Miracles are not for miracles' sake; the Holy Spirit works them through believers in order to turn people to the Lord.

News of Peter's visit to Lydda spread to Joppa, where the Holy Spirit was about to perform an even greater miracle through Peter—the resurrection of Dorcas:

> **Miracles are not for miracles' sake; the Holy Spirit works them through believers in order to turn people to the Lord.**

> **Now there was at Joppa a certain disciple named Tabitha, which by interpretation is called Dorcas: this woman was full of good works and almsdeeds which she did. And it came to pass in those days, that she was sick, and died: whom when they had washed, they laid her in an upper chamber.**

> **Acts 9:36,37**

Dorcas wouldn't lie there for long; the disciples in Joppa sent for Peter. After walking the ten miles from Lydda to Joppa, Peter "...kneeled down, and prayed; and turning him to the body said, Tabitha, arise. And she opened her eyes: and when she saw Peter, she sat up" (Acts 9:40).

Another miracle! And Luke doesn't neglect to tell us the result of this miracle:

> **And it was known throughout all Joppa; and many believed in the Lord. And it came to pass, that he [Peter] tarried many days in Joppa with one Simon a tanner.**

> **Acts 9:42,43**

It was the miraculous that caused many to believe in the Lord. Peter took the opportunity to solidify the new converts' faith by teaching them the Old Testament's prophecies about the Messiah.

At any rate, Peter's stay in Joppa was with a tanner. This interesting fact reveals the breakdown of Peter's strict Jewish upbringing; anyone who handled the hides of clean or unclean animals—namely, tanners—was looked down upon by the Jews. If a woman was betrothed to a man and she found he was a tanner, she could break her betrothal. The Holy Spirit was certainly grooming Peter for the Gentile "Pentecost" at the house of Cornelius!

Gentile Salvation

During the ministry of Jesus on the earth, the disciples were told to take their message only to the Jews:

> **These twelve Jesus sent forth, and commanded them, saying, Go not into the way of the Gentiles, and into any city of the Samaritans enter ye not: but go rather to the lost sheep of the house of Israel.**
>
> **Matthew 10:5,6**

The Jews' rejection of their Messiah opened the way for the Gentiles to participate in God's kingdom:

> **Therefore say I [Jesus] unto you, The kingdom of God shall be taken from you [Jews], and given to a nation bringing forth the fruits thereof.**
>
> **Matthew 21:43**

The Jews' rejection had not taken God by surprise; the Gentiles were prophesied to be a part of God's blessings all along:

And in that day there shall be a root of Jesse, which shall stand for an ensign of the people; to it shall the Gentiles seek: and his rest shall be glorious.

Isaiah 11:10

I the Lord have called thee in righteousness, and will hold thine hand, and will keep thee, and give thee for a covenant of the people, for a light of the Gentiles; to open the blind eyes, to bring out the prisoners from the prison, and them that sit in darkness out of the prison house.

Isaiah 42:6,7

And he said, It is a light thing that thou shouldest be my servant to raise up the tribes of Jacob, and to restore the preserved of Israel: I will also give thee for a light to the Gentiles, that thou mayest be my salvation unto the end of the earth.

Isaiah 49:6

For thou shalt break forth on the right hand and on the left; and thy seed shall inherit the Gentiles, and make the desolate cities to be inhabited.

Isaiah 54:3

Therefore thy gates shall be open continually; they shall not be shut day nor night; that men may bring unto thee the forces of the Gentiles, and that their kings may be brought.

Isaiah 60:11

And I will set a sign among them, and I will send those that escape of them unto the nations, to Tarshish, Pul, and Lud, that draw the bow, to Tubal, and Javan, to the isles afar off, that have not heard my fame, neither have seen my glory; and they shall declare my glory among the Gentiles.

Isaiah 66:19

O Lord, my strength, and my fortress, and my refuge in the day of affliction, the Gentiles shall come unto thee from the ends of the earth, and shall say, Surely our fathers have inherited lies, vanity, and things wherein there is no profit.

Jeremiah 16:19

For from the rising of the sun even unto the going down of the same my name shall be great among the Gentiles; and in every place incense shall be offered unto my name, and a pure offering: for my name shall be great among the heathen, saith the Lord of hosts.

Malachi 1:11

And the scripture, foreseeing that God would justify the heathen through faith, preached before the gospel unto Abraham, saying, In thee shall all nations be blessed.... That the blessing of Abraham might come on the Gentiles through Jesus Christ; that we might receive the promise of the Spirit through faith.

Galatians 3:8,14

For its first eleven years or so, the Church was composed almost exclusively of Jews, but all that was soon to change. Let's take a look at the chronology of the book of Acts.

Acts Time Line

Event	Reference	Approximate Date	Number of Years After Ascension
Ascension	Acts 1	30 A.D.	0
Pentecost	Acts 2	30 A.D.	0
Stephen stoned	Acts 6,7	35 A.D.	5
Paul converted	Acts 9	35 A.D.	5
Cornelius saved	Acts 10	41 A.D.	11
Saul and Barnabus in Antioch	Acts 11	43 A.D.	13
James killed	Acts 12	44 A.D.	14
Paul's first trip; perhaps wrote Galatians at this time	Acts 13	45 A.D.	15
Jerusalem Council	Acts 15	50 A.D.	20
Paul's second trip; at Corinth wrote 1 and 2 Thessalonians	Acts 15	50 A.D.	20
Paul's third trip; at Ephesus wrote 1 and 2 Corinthians; at Corinth wrote Romans	Acts 18	54 A.D.	24
Paul's arrest and trials	Acts 21	58 A.D.	28
Paul's first imprisonment; sent to Rome; wrote Colossians, Philemon, Ephesians, and Philippians	Acts 27	60 A.D.	30
While free, Paul wrote 1 Timothy, Titus, and possibly Hebrews	Acts 27	60 A.D.	30
Paul's second imprisonment; wrote 2 Timothy		67 A.D.	37
Paul's death		67 A.D.	37

The early Church was made up of Jews, but in God's timing, the door was now open to the Gentiles to have equal footing with the Jews in Christ's Church. It would take something spectacular to convince the Jews of God's equal treatment—totally apart from the Law and Jewish traditions—of the Gentiles. The Holy Spirit was the means by which God poured Himself out on Gentile believers.

Peter was the perfect choice to witness the outpouring of the Holy Spirit on the Gentiles, and Cornelius and his household was God's chosen recipients of that gift.

Cornelius lived in Caesarea, which was a Gentile city and the seat of Roman power in Israel. It lies fifty-five miles north of Jerusalem, but on the coast, about one day's journey from Joppa.

God sent an angel to Cornelius while he was praying at the time of the evening sacrifice. Acts 10:4 says of Cornelius, "Thy prayers and thine alms are come up for a memorial before God."

Lasting, *eternal* memorials are built on prayer and deeds of love to those around us. Cornelius was a devout man who put himself in a place where he could hear from God. It is not enough, however, just to *hear* from God—notice that Cornelius was *obedient* to what God told him to do:

And now send men to Joppa, and call for one Simon, whose surname is Peter: he lodgeth with one Simon a tanner, whose house is by the sea side: he shall tell thee what thou oughtest to do.

Acts 10:5,6

The day after God spoke to Cornelius, He prepared Peter for Gentile visitors:

> On the morrow, as they went on their journey, and
> drew nigh unto the city, Peter went up upon the
> housetop to pray about the sixth hour: and he became
> very hungry, and would have eaten: but while they made
> ready, he fell into a trance.

> Acts 10:9,10

Peter saw a sheet filled with unclean animals descending before him, and a voice told him to "kill and eat." Imagine Peter's horror at the prospect of eating animals forbidden by the Mosaic dietary laws! Peter's response was, "Not so, Lord; for I have never eaten any thing that is common or unclean" (Acts 10:14). The voice told Peter, "What God hath cleansed, that call not thou common" (Acts 10:15).

The vision was repeated *three times* to establish it firmly in Peter's thinking. Remember, the Word promises, "In the mouth of two or three witnesses shall every word be established" (2 Cor. 13:1).

The Gentiles were considered "common or unclean" by the Jews, and the Gentile nations were often symbolized by animals in the Bible.

The term *common* is the same word used earlier in the book of Acts in describing the believers who had "all things common" (Acts 4:32). It comes from the Greek word *koinonia,* which means "fellowship" or "in the circle."[7] The Gentiles were considered *outside* the circle.

While Peter pondered the meaning of God's cleansing the unclean or common animals, three men sent from Cornelius knocked on the gate where he was staying. The Holy Spirit told Peter to accompany the three to their Gentile master's house, and Peter obeyed the leading of the Holy Spirit.

Once at Cornelius's house, Peter explained the meaning behind the vision he received from God:

> **And he said undo them, Ye know how that it is an unlawful thing for a man that is a Jew to keep company, or come unto one of another nation; but God hath shewed me that I should not call any man common or unclean.**
>
> Acts 10:28

Peter summed up the whole matter with these words:

> **Of a truth I perceive that God is no respecter of persons: but in every nation he that feareth him, and worketh righteousness, is accepted with him.**
>
> Acts 10:34,35

Peter continued preaching, but his preaching was interrupted:

> **While Peter yet spake these words, the Holy Ghost fell on all them which heard the word. And they of the circumcision which believed were astonished, as many as came with Peter, because that on the Gentiles also was poured out the gift of the Holy Ghost.**
>
> Acts 10:44,45

How shocking for the Jews! Two thousand years of separation from among the other nations suddenly fell away with the outpouring of the Spirit on Jews and Gentiles alike.

Peter was thoroughly convinced of the Spirit's work in the hearts of Cornelius and his household:

> **Can any man forbid water, that these should not be baptized, which have received the Holy Ghost as well as we?**
>
> Acts 10:47

The apostle who had been given the "keys of the kingdom" (Matt. 16:19) used them to unlock the door of salvation and baptism in the Holy Spirit for the Gentiles—but not, as we shall see, without opposition from the Jewish Christians who had comprised the Church up until this time!

When they opposed him, Peter, speaking to the leadership in Jerusalem, had the best defense possible:

> **Forasmuch then as God gave them the like gift** [of the Holy Spirit] **as he did unto us, who believed on the Lord Jesus Christ; what was I, that I could withstand God?**
>
> **Acts 11:17**

> The apostle who had been given the "keys of the kingdom" (Matthew 16:19) used them to unlock the door of salvation and baptism in the Holy Spirit for the Gentiles

"Look brothers," Peter confidently concluded, "this thing was all God from start to finish. The Lord gave me the vision of cleansing the unclean animals, and the Holy Spirit told me to go to Cornelius's house. The Holy Spirit fell on them before I even finished speaking! What else could I do but go along with what God was doing?"

The disciples recognized that Peter did not act on his own but followed the leading of the Holy Spirit, and the way was opened for an historic shift in the direction of the Church:

> **When they heard these things, they held their peace, and glorified God, saying, Then hath God also to the Gentiles granted repentance unto life.**
>
> **Acts 11:18**

Antioch: The New Church Center

The persecution, which began with the stoning of Stephen, scattered believers throughout the region:

> **Now they which were scattered abroad upon the persecution that arose about Stephen travelled as far as Phenice, and Cyprus, and Antioch, preaching the word to none but unto the Jews only.**
>
> **Acts 11:19**

These new Christians preached "the Lord Jesus" (Acts 11:20) to the Jews in the cities where they settled. Luke tells us the results of their preaching in Antioch, the city that was destined to become the new center for Christian evangelism through the apostle Paul:

> **And the hand of the Lord was with them: and a great number believed, and turned unto the Lord.**
>
> **Acts 11:21**

The leadership of the church in Jerusalem eventually heard about the move of the Spirit in Antioch, and they chose Barnabas to go and investigate. What he saw when he got to Antioch must have impressed him! We're told that he was glad, and he exhorted the church there "to cleave unto the Lord" (Acts 11:23).

A strong church will always attract unbelievers into its fold; the light, the joy, and the truth draw them. Antioch was no exception: "and much people was added unto the Lord" (Acts 11:24).

> **A strong church will always attract unbelievers into its fold; the light, the joy, and the truth draw them.**

144

Barnabas was an exhorter, but not much of a teacher. When each part of the Body performs its own function, things run smoothly. Barnabas evidently knew that the new believers in Antioch needed to be grounded in the Word, so he set off for Tarsus to bring back Paul, the master teacher of the Church:

And when he had found him, he brought him unto Antioch. And it came to pass, that a whole year they assembled themselves with the church, and taught much people. And the disciples were called Christians first in Antioch.

Acts 11:26

"Christian" was like a nickname unbelievers gave believers. "They're always preaching Jesus Christ, Jesus Christ, Jesus Christ; they act like they actually know this Jesus Christ!" And so, because of their preaching and witnessing, the Jews and Greeks in the city tagged them with the name "Little Christs."

> We can be so on fire with the Holy Spirit and power that our witness is apparent.

The same can be true of believers today—we can be so on fire with the Holy Spirit and power that our witness is apparent. We *are* little Christs!

Things were so "hot" in Antioch that the leaders in Jerusalem decided to send some of their prophets. Agabus, one of the prophets, foretold of a great famine that would hit Jerusalem and the area of Judea.

Just as Agabus had prophesied, a famine did occur. The saints in Antioch took up a collection to help those in Jerusalem. Now it was the new church's turn to help the parent church. The gift was sent with Barnabas and Paul.

Death and Deliverance

At this time in Church history, Herod Agrippa I, the grandson of Herod the Great, was the Roman ruler over Judea. Herod admired the Jews and wanted to please them, and what better way than to persecute the followers of Jesus! Luke tells us that he killed James, the brother of John, which delighted the Jews. Herod thought, *Well, if the death of James made the Jews happy, Peter's death will make them ecstatic!*

Peter was arrested during the time of Passover. Herod had Peter guarded around the clock by sixteen Roman soldiers, four for each of the four watches throughout the day and night. During each watch, two of the soldiers were chained to Peter while the other two stood guard. Escape was impossible—or so they thought!

Herod didn't expect the Church to take action so fast; this time they prayed with the power of the Holy Spirit:

> **Peter therefore was kept in prison: but prayer was made without ceasing of the church unto God for him.**
>
> **Acts 12:5**

The prayer was "without ceasing," which is from the Greek word *ektenes*, meaning "intense" or "fervent."[8]

The believers prayed day and night for Peter; and when the church prayed, God answered:

> **And, behold, the angel of the Lord came upon him [Peter], and a light shined in the prison: and he smote Peter on the side, and raised him up, saying, Arise up quickly. And his chains fell off from his hands.**
>
> **Acts 12:7**

God has guardian angels that work on His behalf for you and me:

> **But to which of the angels said he at any time, Sit on my right hand, until I make thine enemies thy footstool? Are they not all ministering spirits, sent forth to minister for them who shall be heirs of salvation?**
>
> **Hebrews 1:13,14**

Peter's guardian angel didn't hang around long; he got the job done and departed. After Peter related the details of his release to the disciples, he also is said to have "departed" (Acts 12:17). This is the last we hear about Peter in the book of Acts, with the one exception in Acts 15 at the Jerusalem Council. From here on out, the champion of Christianity would be the apostle Paul.

Before Luke took up the account of Paul's calling and traveled throughout the Roman Empire, he gave us a contrast between the *words of Herod,* which brought death, and the *Word of God,* which brought life:

> **And upon a set day Herod, arrayed in royal apparel, sat upon his throne, and made an oration unto them.... And immediately the angel of the Lord smote him, because he gave not God the glory: and he was eaten of worms, and gave up the ghost. But the Word of God grew and multiplied.**
>
> **Acts 12:21,23,24**

From this point on we shall see the Word of God spread from Antioch into town after town, finally reaching its way to Rome. God always works things out for good: out of the death of James came fervent prayer for Peter; out of the death of Herod the persecutor came the continued growth of the Christian Church and the establishment of a base of operation for a missionary movement unlike anything the world had ever seen! The fire of the Holy Spirit continued to spread, helping the Church share the gospel of Jesus Christ!

Chapter 11

Sticks and Stones

(Acts 13,14)

*H*ow beautifully the gifts and the fruit are shown in this book. In the Jerusalem Council, we see the Holy Spirit is bearing witness and the council's receiving the direction of the Holy Spirit. The Spirit's word of wisdom through Peter and James brought the believers into one accord. (Acts 15:8,9,12-29.) Of course, the Spirit's presence in their midst was sufficient for any problem, and they were willing to give him credit for it.

In Acts 16, we see the wisdom and direction of the Holy Spirit in Paul. His tour goes through Galatia to Troas. The Spirit not only led him, but He also stopped Him when he was going in the wrong direction. (vv.16:6,7.) God directs His children.

We have a number of *firsts* in chapter 13: the first missionary journey of Paul (chapters 13 and 14), the first mention of Saul's name change (v. 9), the first recorded sermon by Paul (v. 16-41), and the first formal turn to the Gentiles with the gospel by Paul and Barnabas (v. 46). Along the way of their gospel mission, we'll encounter a sorcerer who is struck blind, the gathering of an entire city to hear Paul speak, signs and wonders, and even a resurrection!

As we've discussed, the book of Acts is the contemporary Church's standard operating procedure, and Paul's journeys, ministry, and witness are an excellent model for believers today.

In the last verse of chapter 12, we are told that Barnabas and Paul returned to Antioch from their famine-relief trip to Jerusalem. John Mark came back with them, and there was a period of one or two years that Paul and Barnabas ministered to the believers in Antioch. When they had proved their faithfulness, and as they and the others in the church "ministered to the Lord, and fasted" (Acts 13:2), the Holy Spirit called out Barnabas and Paul to begin a missionary movement that is still going on today.

The godly men in leadership in the church at Antioch laid their hands on Barnabas and Paul and sent them out. What a loss those two men must have been to the church there! The church, however, was willing to obey the Holy Spirit and sacrifice for the greater good of God's overall plan of evangelism.

First Stop: Cyprus

On Paul's second and third missionary journeys, he headed north from Antioch into Cilicia and Galatia; but on this first journey with Barnabas, they headed south to the seaport of Seleucia and then set sail to Cyprus.

Verse 5 of this chapter shows us the initial pattern that Barnabas and Paul followed whenever they went into a city:

And when they were at Salamis, they preached the word of God in the synagogues of the Jews: and they had also John to their minister.

Acts 13:5

Salamis must have been a bustling city with more than one synagogue. There was always a time during the Saturday gathering when visitors were acknowledged and given the opportunity to share a greeting and news from other cities.

What a perfect setup! Luke tells us that Barnabas and Paul preached the Word of God to the Jews. We're also told that John Mark came along to minister to Barnabas and Paul. "Minister" is the Greek word *huperetes,* which is a nautical term meaning "a rower on a ship."[9] John Mark came along to provide for the personal needs of the apostles.

Barnabas, Paul, and John Mark walked the length of the island, preaching as they went. They finally ended up at the city of Paphos on the southwestern end of the isle. A temple to Venus, the goddess of love, stood in or near Paphos; she was worshiped as the "Queen of Paphos." Once during her lifetime every woman in Cyprus was required to offer herself in prostitution at the temple. The money from this abominable practice went to further the worship of Venus and to the priests who were the custodians of the temple. This was the heathen society into which Paul and Barnabus took the gospel!

Rome governed the island of Cyprus from the city of Paphos. The proconsul in charge was one Sergius Paulus. Obviously this man had some kind of interest in the things of God, or he would not have sent for Barnabas and Paul and desired to hear the Word of God from their lips.

Opposition to the gospel message came from a backslidden Jew named Bar-Jesus, who evidently had some kind of association with the proconsul. Bar-Jesus also went by the name *Elymas* which means "a wizard."[10] Far from being enlightened, this Jew had turned his back on the light of God found in His Word. Bar-Jesus actively sought to turn Sergius Paulus away from the truth taught by Barnabas and Paul, but he had never met anyone like Paul:

Then Saul, (who also is called Paul,) filled with the Holy Ghost, set his eyes on him, and said, O full of all subtilty and all mischief, thou child of the devil, thou enemy of all righteousness, wilt thou not cease to pervert the right ways of the Lord?

Acts 13:9,10

Paul was not about to be intimidated by anyone of any rank, position, or persuasion. Speaking by the inspiration of the Holy Spirit, Paul pronounced blindness for a season upon the "enlightened" one. This miracle confirmed the gospel message preached by Paul and Barnabas and resulted in the salvation of Sergius Paulus—the "prudent" Roman governor of Cyprus! (Acts 13:7.) Paul's willingness to follow the leading of his Helper, the Holy Spirit, brought much fruit to the Church.

The Church in Turkey

Acts 13:13 mentions Paul "and his company" leaving Cyprus and crossing over into what is modern-day Turkey. From this point on it is Paul who is usually mentioned ahead of Barnabas in the narrative. They landed at Perga, which was the capital city of the region of Pamphylia. It was here that John Mark departed from Paul and Barnabas and returned to his home in Jerusalem.

We are simply not told the reasons for John Mark's defection, but whatever the reason, his departure would later create serious contention between Paul and Barnabas and would eventually lead to their separation.

Leaving Perga, Paul and Barnabas traveled to Pisidia, Antioch, another capital city. As was their custom, Paul and Barnabas went to the synagogue and waited for their opportunity to speak. Sure enough, the rulers of the synagogue asked them if they had any word of exhortation. (Acts 13:15.) Paul wasted no time with pleasantries but dove into a lengthy recap of Jewish history, leading right down to John the Baptist and Jesus Himself.

Paul's message ended with some hard words about the Law of Moses and a warning against rejecting the forgiveness being offered:

> **Be it known unto you therefore, men and brethren, that through this man is preached unto you the forgiveness of sins: and by him all that believe are justified from all things, from which ye could not be justified by the law of Moses. Beware therefore, lest that come upon you, which is spoken of in the prophets; behold, ye despisers, and wonder, and perish: for I work a work in your days, a work which ye shall in no wise believe, though a man declare it unto you.**
>
> **Acts 13:38-41**

As always, there were two reactions to Paul's preaching. In this instance, most of those who were of pure Jewish blood left the synagogue in a huff, while some Jews and the Gentile proselytes to Judaism wanted to hear more about Jesus. The news about Paul and his gospel spread throughout the town, and the following Saturday "almost the whole city" gathered to hear Paul preach. (Acts 13:44.)

When the Jews saw the multitude that followed after Paul and Barnabas, the Scripture says that envy moved them to argue against the truth and actually blaspheme God.

The Turn to the Gentiles

The Jews' stiff-necked rejection produced a dramatic turning point in the apostles' ministry:

Then Paul and Barnabas waxed bold, and said, It was necessary that the word of God should first have been spoken to you: but seeing ye put it from you, and judge yourselves unworthy of everlasting life, lo, we turn to the Gentiles.

Acts 13:46

The Holy Spirit brought a quote from the prophet Isaiah to Paul's mind and gave him fresh direction and inspiration for his God-given mission:

For so hath the Lord commanded us, saying, I have set thee to be a light of the Gentiles, that thou shouldest be for salvation unto the ends of the earth.

Acts 13:47

Naturally this made the Gentiles happy:

And when the Gentiles heard this, they were glad, and glorified the word of the Lord: and as many as were ordained to eternal life believed. And the word of the Lord was published throughout all the region.

Acts 13:48,49

Likewise, hardships and adverse circumstances could not affect the inward peace and happiness that Paul and Barnabas had found in their relationship with the living God. Acts 13:52 says, "And the disciples were filled with joy, and with the Holy Ghost."

On to Iconium

Despite turning to the Gentiles, Paul and Barnabas once again used the forum of the Jewish synagogue to spread their message at Iconium, the capital of a region known as Lycaonia. Their ministry was so powerful and persuasive in the Holy Spirit that "a great multitude both of the Jews and also of the Greeks believed" (Acts 14:1).

The unbelieving Jews, however, once again stirred up opposition; but this time the Lord performed signs and wonders through the hands of Paul and Barnabas to confirm His message and His messengers.

Eventually the city was sharply divided into two camps: believers and unbelievers. The apostles were made aware of a plot to stone them. They could have stayed and relied on the Lord's protection, but they chose to take their message to Lystra, a city composed largely of Gentile idolaters. No mention is made of Paul and Barnabas's preaching in the Jewish synagogues in Lystra or Derbe, and their ministry was met with acceptance at both towns.

It was at Lystra that we have the first recorded time the gift of healing worked through Paul:

> **And there sat a certain man at Lystra, impotent in his feet, being a cripple from his mother's womb, who never had walked: the same heard Paul speak: who stedfastly beholding him, and perceiving that he had faith to be healed, said with a loud voice, Stand upright on thy feet. And he leaped and walked.**
>
> **Acts 14:8-10**

As a result of this miracle, Paul and Barnabas faced an entirely different problem than they had experienced in Antioch or Icoruum: the pagan crowd tried to worship and offer sacrifices to them! The citizens of Lystra worshiped the planets and had their own temple to Jupiter. Paul refused their worship and took the opportunity to speak against the vain practice of worshiping the creation instead of the Creator:

> **Sirs, why do ye these things? We also are men of like passions with you, and preach unto you that ye should turn from these vanities unto the living God, which made heaven, and earth, and the sea, and all things that are therein.**
>
> **Acts 14:15**

The people would have been willing to hear more from Paul and Barnabas, but Jews from Antioch and Iconium were so enraged at Paul that they followed him to Lystra and turned the people against him:

> **And there came thither certain Jews from Antioch and Iconium, who persuaded the people and, having**

stoned Paul, drew him out of the city, supposing he had been dead.

Acts 14:19

Bible scholars have a difference of opinion as to whether Paul was actually dead at this time or merely unconscious. I personally believe he was dead. A group of disciples stood around Paul, praying for him, and Luke tells us that he rose up and was taken back into the city. The Greek word for "rose up" is *anistemi,* and it is used 111 times in the New Testament with around 35 of those instances referring to bodily resurrection.[11]

Nevertheless, Paul's resurrection was absolutely supernatural. How do I know? Because verse 20 says that the very next day he headed out with Barnabas to Derbe, some eighteen miles away by foot!

Paul was neither intimidated by his persecutors nor reluctant to speak out for fear of offending his listeners. He was bold in the Spirit! As soon as he and Barnabas arrived in Derbe they "preached the gospel to that city" (Acts 14:21). After they finished making disciples in Derbe, they headed right back to Lystra! Paul cared more about the saints than the stones, retracing his steps so that he could strengthen the new believers in their faith amidst a hostile culture.

The Holy Spirit brings boldness and victory, but we have to become His willing prisoners. We have to accept the boundaries He sets forth and His constraints, because they are necessary for His purposes.

Chapter 12

Decision Time

(*Acts 15:1-35*)

cts 15 is one of the most important chapters in the book of Acts. The issue decided at what is commonly known as the "Jerusalem Council" has been a foundation throughout the Church age. The contention was so strong that it easily could have divided the New Testament Church into two factions of Jewish and Gentile believers. Verse 1 tells us the crux of the matter:

> **And certain men which came down from Judaea taught the brethren, and said, Except ye be circumcised after the manner of Moses, ye cannot be saved.**
>
> **Acts 15:1**

Paul made reference to these men in his letter to the Galatians:

For before that certain came from James, he [Peter]
did eat with the Gentiles: but when they were come, he
withdrew and separated himself, fearing them which
were of the circumcision.

Galatians 2:12

Imagine the influence these visitors had: they were from
Jerusalem, the "mother" church, and they came in the name of
James, one of the leading apostles of the church and the half-
brother of Jesus. These Jewish believers were teaching that if the
Gentiles were not circumcised, they were not saved.

The church at Antioch was a very free church, having both born-
again Jews *and* Gentiles as members. They moved together, they
flowed together, they had the same vision for the kingdom, but
when the visitors arrived from the church in Jerusalem, the Jewish
believers at Antioch refused to eat with their Gentile brothers and
sisters. The Jewish believers held on to the ritual requirements of the
Mosaic Law, and it became a very serious situation in the church at
Antioch—with repercussions for the Church worldwide.

Faith Plus Works

The principle under attack here was salvation by faith alone. It
was a conflict between faith *plus* circumcision or faith without
circumcision. It was a conflict between the ritual law and the spiritual law and a conflict between flesh and spirit. It brought much
dissension because it attempted to mix grace with the Law. Paul
saw the seriousness of it in overturning the purity of God's purpose
in sending Jesus to the Cross. There was strong dissension, and it
looked like there could be an insurrection in the Church.

Watch how the Holy Spirit brings unity to the church. The outpouring of the Holy Spirit changed the direction of the Church and broke down the walls of prejudice.

The Samaritans, whom the Jews considered less than dirt, received the outpouring of the Holy Spirit. The Jews viewed the Gentiles as dogs. If the devil can get Christians to fight among themselves, they will have no energy to reach the world for Christ. It is the enemy's favorite tactic, and it is still used today in the Christian Church.

> **If the devil can get Christians to fight among themselves, they will have no energy to reach the world for Christ.**

The Antioch church finally decided that the matter would have to be solved in Jerusalem by the apostles and elders. Paul and Barnabas went to Jerusalem and declared the wonderful things that God had been doing among the Gentiles, or the uncircumcised:

> **Then all the multitude kept silence, and gave audience to Barnabas and Paul, declaring what miracles and wonders God had wrought among the Gentiles by them.**
>
> **Acts 15:12**

The Gentiles had been saved without the rite of circumcision. The Jewish teachers who were teaching that the Gentiles had to be circumcised in order to be saved were born-again Pharisees. They believed in Jesus as Messiah, but they were very legalistic. They had missed the spirit of the Law:

> **For circumcision verily profiteth, if thou keep the law: but if thou be a breaker of the law, thy circumcision is made uncircumcision.**

Therefore if the uncircumcision keep the righteousness of the law, shall not his uncircumcision be counted
for circumcision? And shall not uncircumcision which is
by nature, if it fulfil the law, judge thee, who by the letter
and circumcision dost transgress the law?

For he is not a Jew, which is one outwardly; neither is
that circumcision, which is outward in the flesh: but he
is a Jew, which is one inwardly; and circumcision is that
of the heart, in the spirit, and not in the letter; whose
praise is not of men, but of God.

Romans 2:25-29

If you look at the attack that Satan was trying to make, you can
see that the Church could have died right at this point. If they had
made the decision that all Gentiles had to be circumcised and had
to keep the Mosaic Law, that would have been the end of the
Church. The Church would simply have been a small group of
Jewish believers.

Time was very short. This conference at Jerusalem took place
around 50 A.D., and within the next eight years Paul was arrested.
Shortly after that would be the great fire of Rome, and Nero would
use Christians as scapegoats—they would be persecuted ruth-
lessly. In 70 A.D. the destruction of Jerusalem would be completed.
If the Gentile world was not evangelized quickly, there would have
been no strong foundation from which to grow outside Jerusalem.

When Paul and Barnabas arrived in Jerusalem, I am sure they
were looked upon with skepticism, even though Paul had been
there before (this was his third visit to Jerusalem). Certainly Paul
understood the Pharisees because he had been one. The Pharisees
believed in resurrection, so it probably was not too difficult for
them to believe in the resurrection of Jesus. The Sadducees did not

believe in a resurrection of any kind, so it was harder for Sadducees to become believers, but the converted Pharisees seemed to remain legalistic at heart and were becoming a Jewish sect in the Christian Church.

Peter to the Defense

Peter, who was sent to the circumcised (the Jews), gave one of the best arguments *against* circumcision. Peter shared the full testimony of his preaching and teaching in the home of Cornelius. (Acts 10.) Peter told how the baptism of the Holy Spirit was given to the Gentiles just as it was to the Jews. God had not distinguished between them; their hearts were purified by faith.

In Acts 15:10, Peter said that the Law was a yoke of bondage. Jesus had said, "Take my yoke upon you.... For my yoke is easy, and my burden is light" (Matt. 11:29,30).

Paul taught the Galatians about the yoke of bondage:

Stand fast therefore in the liberty wherewith Christ hath made us free, and be not entangled again with the yoke of bondage.

Galatians 5:1

When we come to Jesus, we find out that the law of circumcision was a yoke of bondage to the flesh. But when we take His yoke, we have the yoke of His grace. The Jews were saved by faith, and the Gentiles were saved by faith. It was a work of the Holy Spirit.

The rabbis continued to add little pieces of law to the commandments until they became such a load that no man could carry them. Paul even told about how he could not keep the tenth commandment concerning evil desires. (Rom. 7:15-23.) Only Jesus kept the Law. If all of these burdens had been put upon the Gentiles, it would have driven them to destruction.

Peter's question was, "Why should the Church fasten on the new Gentile believers' shoulders the yoke of the Law? Jesus came to set them free. The Jews have never been able to do it; how could they expect the Gentiles to keep the Law?" The Law puts the load on man, but grace puts the load on Christ. The two can never be compatible.

After Peter testified (verse 12), Barnabas and Paul began. Of course, they had seen firsthand what was happening among the Gentiles. They knew that God was at work mightily. Paul, who had been the greatest legalist of all, received the greatest revelation of grace. We can still read his words concerning grace in Romans 4 and in the book of Galatians.

Paul spoke of Abraham, the father of all who believed. Before Abraham was circumcised, God had given him the promise. Before Abraham received circumcision, and even *after* Abraham received circumcision, he walked in faith, and this was not the Abrahamic covenant; this was the new covenant:

> **That the blessing of Abraham might come on the Gentiles through Jesus Christ; that we might receive the promise of the Spirit through faith.**
>
> **Galatians 3:14**

Paul later had Timothy circumcised (Acts 16:3), and yet he did not allow Titus to be circumcised (Gal. 2:3). He gave his reasons for this:

> **And unto the Jews I became as a Jew, that I might gain the Jews; to them that are under the law, as under the law, that I might gain them that are under the law; to them that are without law, as without law, (being not**

without law to God, but under the law to Christ,) that I might gain them that are without law.

1 Corinthians 9:20,21

Then James spoke with much importance on God's Word. (v. 13-21.). He quoted from Amos 9:11-12. Peter had quoted from Joel on the Day of Pentecost, showing the Jews the prophecy of the outpouring of the Holy Spirit. James quoted from Amos, showing the Jews that the outpouring of the Holy Spirit on the Gentiles had placed them in the new covenant. Amos had prophesied that God would again build the tabernacle of David so that the Gentiles would come into it:

And to this agree the words of the prophets; as it is written, After this I will return, and will build again the tabernacle of David, which is fallen doom; and I will build again the ruins thereof, and I will set it up: that the residue of men might seek after the Lord, and all the Gentiles, upon whom my name is called, saith the Lord, who doeth all these things.

Acts 15:15-17

The Tabernacle of Moses or David

The Jews had been under the Mosaic covenant and they knew the tabernacle of Moses, but the Gentiles would not come into the tabernacle of *Moses* (which represented the Law); they would come into the tabernacle of *David.* They were coming into the newer covenant by faith in the son of David, Jesus Christ.

The tabernacle of David has a most interesting history. In 1 Chronicles chapters 15-17, we see that David established a new order of worship in the tabernacle. He placed the tabernacle at Mount Zion. The tabernacle of Moses had been at Mount Gibeon, but David moved it. So the tabernacle of Moses still had priests who ministered there, but now David had other priests who were ministering at his tabernacle. David had taken the ark of the covenant out of the tabernacle of Moses and placed it in his tabernacle—the tabernacle of David. We know that the ark of the covenant typified God's glory; thus the glory had been removed from the Mosaic tabernacle and put into David's tabernacle.

The outpouring of the Holy Spirit on the Gentiles was God's seal that they had already believed in Christ. There was a new order of worship in David's tabernacle. There was singing and praising and joy and thanksgiving. The tabernacle of Moses simply had its outer-court functions. The priest couldn't go into the Holy of Holies—there was no ark of the covenant. The great sacrifices of David's tabernacle were the sacrifices of praise.

All this has a parallel in the New Testament. When Jesus died, the veil of the temple was torn in two:

And, behold, the veil of the temple was rent in twain from the top to the bottom; and the earth did quake, and the rocks rent.

Matthew 27:51

This showed that God's presence had changed to His new place of habitation—to the Church, the temple of the living God, built up with living stones. The Helper that Jesus promised had come to live in the lives of all believers who would accept Him.

I absolutely love the way James was able to quote from the little book of Amos to verify what Paul and Barnabas shared concerning the salvation of the Gentiles. The salvation of Cornelius's household in Acts 10 was the fulfillment of Amos's prophecy regarding the reestablishment of David's tabernacle and the coming in of the Gentiles to God's house by faith apart from the Law.

The Gentiles were indeed turning to God, but earlier James had pointed out that it was God who was choosing the Gentiles to become a part of the Church:

> **Simeon hath declared how God at the first did visit the Gentiles, to take out of them a people for his name.**
>
> **Acts 15:14**

That's what the Church is all about— God's calling out a people for His name. The word *ekklesia* means a "called out assembly."[12] God has a calling-out process. It began at Pentecost with the Jews. Then He called out Cornelius's household, and He continued with other Gentiles. Paul and Barnabas had gone to the land of the Gentiles, calling out people for God's Church. God is still calling out Jews and Gentiles; they are His Church.

This showed that God's presence had changed to His new place of habitation—to the Church, the temple of the living God, built up with living stones.

James's decree was that the Gentiles had come into the Body of Christ apart from the Law and thus were not under the yoke of circumcision. They were not under the Mosaic covenant; they were in the new covenant—the way of salvation, which is faith in Christ Jesus.

Finally, circumcision is to be of the heart of both Jew and Gentile—and that comes through the Holy Spirit, who sets apart *believers* for the Master's use. Paul wrapped up the argument against believers' fleshly circumcision by saying, "If ye be led of the Spirit, ye are not under the law" (Gal. 5:18). Thus he declared the new dispensation by which believers were to live—not according to the Law *but according to the Spirit of God.*

Now, the Church knew the truth: true circumcision was of the heart and not of the flesh. Acts 7:8 speaks of the "covenant of circumcision" that God made with Abraham. In the New Testament the covenant of circumcision is a covenant in the heart and in the spirit, but not in the flesh and of the letter. God looks for the new creature, the one whose heart has been circumcised:

Therefore if any man be in Christ, he is a new creature: old things are passed away; behold, all things are become new.
2 Corinthians 5:17

God looks for the new creature, the one whose heart has been circumcised.

The Holy Spirit performs spiritual circumcision in our hearts:

In whom also ye are circumcised with the circumcision made without hands, in putting off the body of the sins of the flesh by the circumcision of Christ: buried with him in baptism, wherein also ye are risen with him through the faith of the operation of God, who hath raised him from the dead.
Colossians 2:11,12

From the human standpoint, the Church had passed a crucial test. From God's viewpoint, the outcome was sure all along because Jesus had said, "I will build my church; and the gates of hell shall not prevail against it" (Matt. 16:18).

Notice how Paul was willing to trust the Holy Spirit in this matter. In the natural no one would have thought that the leadership in Jerusalem would abandon its strong legalistic ways. God is bigger than all the plans of men. Like Paul, we can trust in the leading of the Holy Spirit and know that God's Word will emerge triumphant in every situation.

Now that the Church was one and with the help of the Holy Spirit, the gospel would be taken into a new continent—Europe. Paul's second missionary journey is filled with the supernatural: demons cast out, a great earthquake, and the conversion of an entire household in the middle of the night!

Chapter 13

The Gospel Goes to Europe

(Acts 15:36-16:40)

Paul could have stayed in Antioch and built a thriving ministry there, but his heart was with the men, women, and children whose faces he remembered from his first missionary journey. Paul loved the churches he had begun; he spoke of their care in his letter to the Corinthians:

> **Beside those things that are without, that which cometh upon me daily, the care of all the churches.**
>
> **2 Corinthians 11:28**

Paul had founded the churches and they were his children. He and Barnabas began to make preparations to retrace the steps of their first trip abroad with the gospel, but they came into sharp contention because Paul did not want John Mark to accompany them again. Instead, Paul took Silas with him. Silas was a "chief man" among the church in Jerusalem. (Acts 15:22.)

All four men—Paul, Silas, Barnabas, and Mark—were sent forth by the church with the grace of God. (Acts 15:40.) God's grace would work in them all. Paul and Silas went through Syria and Cilicia, confirming the churches. The churches were thriving.

Timothy Joins the Team

When they arrived at Lystra, Paul encountered Timothy, a very promising young man who had been converted when Paul and Barnabas traveled through Lystra on the first missionary trip.

Timothy was the son of a Jewish mother and a Greek father. It appears that his mother, Eunice, and Lois, his grandmother, had raised Timothy. Both were godly women; consequently, Timothy was brought up more as a Jew than a Gentile.

Lystra, Timothy's hometown, was the place where Paul was stoned on his first missionary journey. It is interesting that when Stephen was stoned, Paul became the fruit of Stephen's stoning. Paul was stoned at Lystra, and it appears that Timothy became the fruit of Paul's stoning.

Timothy had proved himself faithful in a local church before Paul took him along to train him and to use him in ministry. Timothy received his ministry through prophecy and the laying on of hands:

This charge I commit unto thee, son Timothy, according to the prophecies which went before on thee, that thou by them mightest war a good warfare.

1 Timothy 1:18

Neglect not the gift that is in thee, which was given thee by prophecy, with the laying on of the hands of the presbytery.

1 Timothy 4:14

Wherefore I put thee in remembrance that thou stir up the gift of God, which is in thee by the putting on of my hands.

2 Timothy 1:6

Circumcision or Uncircumcision?

The Jerusalem Council had decided that circumcision was *not* a requirement for Gentiles to be saved. Paul stood firmly on the side of those who came to that conclusion. Why then, many people ask, did Paul have Timothy circumcised? Because he was not circumcised though his mother was a Jewess, Timothy in a sense was neither Jew nor Gentile. Paul felt that it was good to have Timothy circumcised so that he could minister to the Jews alongside Paul. It wasn't that circumcision was a requirement to preach the gospel—but it did make for more openness on the part of the Jews when Paul and Timothy spoke:

For though I be free from all men, yet have I made myself servant unto all, that I might gain the more. And unto the Jews I became as a Jew, that I might gain the

> **Jews; to them that are under the law, as under the law; that I might gain them that are under the law.**
>
> **1 Corinthians 9:19,20**

As Paul, Silas, and Timothy began their trip, we read about their search for the leading of the Holy Spirit. Acts 16:6 says they were "forbidden" of the Holy Spirit to go to Asia and the Spirit "suffered them not" to go into the region of Bithynia. (Acts 16:7.) The Holy Spirit has to prepare people's hearts before the Word can be effectively preached, and it was not the right time. Paul did not try to force the issue; he just listened to the Holy Spirit. There are timings for cities as well as timings for people.

That's an important thing for us to remember: God may have laid something on our hearts, but unless we listen to the leading of the Holy Spirit, we can still miss God's plan, but when we listen to His guidance, He will lead us into the perfect plan in God's perfect timing.

God may have laid something on our hearts, but unless we listen to the leading of the Holy Spirit, we can still miss God's plan, unless we listen to His guidance.

Paul seemed to be constantly leading his team westward, always listening for the still, small voice of the Holy Spirit. We always have to follow the Lord of the harvest, because He knows where the harvest is!

When Paul arrived at Troas, an important city with a harbor that linked Macedonia, Greece, and Europe, he stopped. This was a strategic place, and Paul needed to hear from the Holy Spirit where to go next. The Holy Spirit spoke to Paul in a vision in the night; a man from Macedonia called Paul to come over and help him. This later proved to be a turning point in Church history. Paul traveled westward into Europe, and the fires of evangelism spread quickly through the West. If Paul had gone eastward, India and China would have been first. God chose the path for the gospel.

Notice that Paul obeyed the leading of the Holy Spirit *immediately:*

And after he had seen the vision, immediately we endeavoured to go into Macedonia, assuredly gathering that the Lord had called us for to preach the gospel unto them.

Acts 16:10

In other words, once you've got the direction from the Holy Spirit, you can *move!*

Luke Joins the Team

The "we" in Acts 16:10 must include Luke, the author of Acts. This is the first mention of "we," and many Bible scholars feel that Luke must have joined Paul's team during the stay over in Troas. The group left Troas and stopped overnight at Samothracia, an island that jutted up out of the Aegean Sea to a height of 5,000 feet. It was midway between Troas and Neapolis, which was the seaport serving the city of Philippi, some ten miles inland.

> In other words, once you've got the direction from the Holy Spirit, you can *move!*

Philippi was a colonial city, an outpost of the Roman Empire. Rome ruled the world through her colonies.

First Converts in Europe

On the first Sabbath day after he arrived, Paul went outside the city to a riverside area used for worship. God opened the heart of a woman he met there—the first European convert to Christianity—and she in turn opened her house to Paul's missionary team. Notice that Lydia's conversion was part of a *household* salvation:

> **And when she was baptized, and her household, she besought us, saying, If ye have judged me to be faithful to the Lord, come into my house, and abide there. And she constrained us.**
>
> **Acts 16:15**

Paul's second convert in Europe was a demon-possessed girl. We turn from Lydia, a cultured businesswoman, to a captive slave, a demon-possessed girl. The gospel can make a difference in every person's life.

The girl had a spirit of *divination,* which is translated from the Greek word *python,* meaning a huge serpent.[13] This demon-possessed girl made so-called inspired utterances. Those who owned her used her to tell fortunes. She was very valuable to them, and she was entirely at their mercy. Hers was a pitiful, pitiful state.

She followed Paul and his company, crying out after them. Paul didn't minister to her right away; he waited awhile and then cast the spirits out of her. The girl was instantly set free! She no longer had any ability to give evil prophecies or tell fortunes, and her masters were furious.

Only twice in the book of Acts do we see Gentiles persecuting Paul and the Church, and both times the persecution arose over the issue of money. This time the girl's owners became irate when they saw that their livelihood had been taken from them. (Acts 15:19.)

The apostles were terribly beaten:

And the multitude rose up together against them: and the magistrates rent off their clothes, and commanded to beat them. And when they had laid many stripes upon them, they cast them into prison...and made their feet fast in the stocks.

Acts 16:22-25

The Philippian Jailer Believers

Despite their "stripes" and stocks, Paul and Silas sang praises to God in the night. The prisoners heard them and were all delivered! God sent a very *intelligent* earthquake—it didn't kill anyone; it only shook up the place and loosened the chains of the prisoners and the doors of the prisons. By their worship and praise, Paul and Silas set the atmosphere for the Holy Spirit to move, and move He did!

Three miracles happened here: Paul and Silas rejoiced in their suffering, the earthquake opened every door and loosened every chain, and no prisoner ran off. If the prisoners had escaped, the Roman government would have killed the jailer on duty. When the jailer was awakened out of his sleep and saw the doors opened, he was ready to kill himself.

With the help of the Holy Spirit, Paul knew of the jailer's intentions and intervened, telling the jailer not to commit suicide. Immediately, the man wanted to be saved! In fact, he and his whole family came to Christ. Ironically, the one who had given Paul and Silas their stripes now *washed* their stripes:

And he took them the same hour of the night, and washed their stripes; and was baptized, he and all his, straightway.

Acts 16:33

I love Paul's boldness. When he was released from the jail, he invoked the legal rights he had as a Roman citizen rather than simply leaving town quietly:

But Paul said unto them, They have beaten us openly uncondemned, being Romans, and have cast us into prison; and now do they thrust us out privily? nay verily; but let them come themselves and fetch us out.

Acts 16:37

After being brought out of prison, Paul and Silas brought comfort to the new local church, which was in the house of Lydia. (Acts 16:40.)

Paul later wrote to the church he began in Philippi. You would think that his memories of this town would be negative—the beating, the stocks, and the public humiliation—but the church in Philippi was born as a result of the miraculous, and the epistle to the Philippians is filled with joy and rejoicing!

Here again we see the supernatural operation of the Holy Spirit. The believers in Philippi should have been comforting Paul and Silas after their ordeal; instead, the Holy Spirit supernaturally strengthened Paul and Silas to bring comfort and encouragement to the saints in Lydia's house.

Not one to lie around bathing his wounds, Paul departed from Philippi to find new souls who hadn't yet heard the gospel. The Holy Spirit lead him to Thessalonica, Berea, Athens, and eventually Corinth, where Paul would spend one-and-a-half years and write two vitally important New Testament letters to the church at Thessalonica.

Chapter 14

Unknown Gods and Know-It-All Athenians

(Acts 17)

In Acts 17 we see Paul on the road, passing through the two small towns of Amphipolis and Apollonia. His first destination was the largest population center and the chief seaport of Macedonia—Thessalonica.

As in every place he visited, Paul began preaching in the synagogue. Paul taught there for three Sabbaths before being forced to leave. His stay in Thessalonica may have been longer than three weeks; perhaps he taught privately in homes for almost six months. We know that Paul supported himself by making tents.

A great multitude believed:

> **And some of them believed, and consorted with Paul and Silas; and of the devout Greeks a great multitude, and of the chief women not a few.**
>
> **Acts 17:4**

These "devout Greeks" were Greek-speaking Jews. They accepted the apostles because Paul was a well-schooled rabbi, Silas was from Jerusalem, and Timothy was a half-Jew who had been circumcised by Paul. Paul mentioned the Thessalonians' openness in his first letter to them:

> **For this cause also thank we God without ceasing, because, when ye received the word of God which ye heard of us, ye received it not as the word of men, but as it is in truth, the word of God, which effectually worketh also in you that believe.**
>
> **1 Thessalonians 2:13**

Revivals and Riots

There was opposition wherever Paul preached. It seemed that two things always followed Paul—revivals and riots. The envious Jews charged Paul with turning the world upside down, but it was the unbelieving Jews' jealousy of Paul's success in evangelizing the multitude that caused the riots. These Jews stirred up the crowds and stormed the house where Paul and his company were staying.

Paul hurried away by night to Berea—some sixty miles away. This was evidently the last time Paul was physically in Thessalonica:

Wherefore we would have come unto you, even I Paul, once and again; but Satan hindered us.

1 Thessalonians 2:18

As you study the books of Thessalonians, you'll find that although this church was subject to persecution, it stayed true to God. Because Paul was hindered from returning, he wrote two letters to them. Sometimes what seems like a failure can turn out to be a blessing. Satan's hindering resulted in two wonderful letters that still speak to millions today!

Despite their treatment in Thessalonica, Paul, Silas, and Timothy went directly to the synagogue in Berea. The Jews there were very eager to study the Word. They were neither hard-hearted, closed, prejudiced, nor gullible. They searched the Word and many believed.

When the Jews from Thessalonica heard that Paul was preaching in Berea and having success, they made the sixty-mile trip by foot to stir up opposition once again. Imagine their hatred for Paul to make such a long trip on foot! The Jews' hatred seemed primarily directed toward Paul, not Silas or Timothy. Paul left Berea immediately, following the words of Jesus, which the Holy Spirit brought to his heart:

> **Satan's hindering resulted in two wonderful letters that still speak to millions today!**

But when they persecute you in this city, flee ye into another.

Matthew 10:23

Silas and Timothy were able to remain in Berea while Paul set sail for Athens—the sophisticated, academic center of the world.

This would be a whole new group of people, drastically different from the Greek Jews of Thessalonica and Berea.

Paul in Athens

The Parthenon of Athens (the temple dedicated to the virgin Athena, the goddess of wisdom and the arts) sat atop a hill, the Acropolis, and overlooked the whole city. Whereas Jerusalem was the religious center of that day and Rome the political center, Athens was the architectural, cultural, and intellectual center.

Antioch, Tarsus, Ephesus, and Alexandria were also hubs of philosophic learning—but nothing akin to Athens. Philosophers like Socrates, Plato, and Aristotle were centered at Athens. It also was literally a center of idols. It is said that there were nearly 3,000 idols in the city of Athens!

The Greeks gave us much—a love of knowledge, a love of beauty, and a love of freedom—but spiritually, they were bankrupt. They would find many truths, but never *the truth*. As usual, Paul took his message to the synagogue first:

> **Therefore disputed he in the synagogue with the Jews, and with the devout persons, and in the market daily with them that met with him.**
>
> **Acts 17:17**

Paul wasn't a tourist; he was a missionary. His preaching was not confined to the Jewish synagogue; he took his message to the Agora, or central marketplace of Athens.

Verse 18 requires some explanation:

> **Then certain philosophers of the Epicureans, and of the Stoicks, encountered him. And some said, What will**

this babbler say? other some, He seemeth to be a setter forth of strange gods: because he preached unto them Jesus, and the resurrection.

Acts 17:18

The Epicureans were of a certain school of philosophy that had been founded by the thinker Epicures (342-270 B.C.). They believed that indulgence was the key to life. We derive our word *epicure* (a person who has a fine taste for food and drink) from this philosophy.

The Epicureans felt that there were gods but that the gods had no interest in mankind. Therefore man's chief end was to seek pleasure in this life—because there was no resurrection or life after death.

The Stoics were in many ways the opposite. They were followers of a man named Zeno of Cyprus (340 to 260 B.C.). Although they, too, denied any resurrection, their main belief centered on living a life free of passion, joy, grief, pain, or pleasure. Indifference was to be the key to life. They were basically stern and impassive.

These two groups of philosophers came together to confront Paul and his teaching. Some called Paul a "babbler." The word *babbler* comes from the Greek word *spermologos,* a small bird that picks up seed along the road.[1] In other words, Paul was being called a "scrap picker," someone who just picked up this teaching and that but nothing that would really appeal to an intelligent person.

Other Athenians sneered at the gospel and said that Paul seemed to be a proclaimer of "strange gods." The word for "gods" is *daimonion,* which is usually translated as "devil" or "demons."[15] With such hostility to the gospel, it is no wonder that there was no substantial church established in Athens until two hundred years after Paul's visit!

These intellectuals took Paul to the Areopagus (a limestone hill between the Acropolis and the Agora), which was also known as Mars Hill. This was where the temple of Mars stood and the court of the Areopagus convened. This was a civil court that actually exercised a great deal of authority over people like Paul.

The Athenians were always open to some new kind of philosophy. They spent their leisure hours picking up bits of news, looking for new philosophies and new, so-called intellectual interests. We would say that *they* were the seed pickers! Paul stood boldly and preached the gospel; he was a soul winner at heart. Let's take a close look at Paul's presentation to these intellectual Athenians:

> **Then Paul stood in the midst of Mars' hill, and said, Ye men of Athens, I perceive that in all things ye are too superstitious.**
>
> **Acts 17:22**

The Greek phrase for "too superstitious" might be better translated "deeply religious" or "religiously disposed." Although it might sound like it, Paul did not begin his sermon by insulting his listeners—he was wiser than that.

> **For as I passed by, and beheld your devotions, I found an altar with this inscription, TO THE UNKNOWN GOD. Whom therefore ye ignorantly worship, him declare I unto you.**
>
> **Acts 17:23**

Their "devotions" were actually the idols they worshiped. Paul called attention to the god that they worshiped called "Agnostos," the *unknown*. They knew everything that could be humanly known in that day, but they didn't know God.

Now, with the Jews, Paul always reasoned using the Scriptures, but with these Gentiles, he reasoned using creation as his example:

> **God that made the world and all things therein, seeing that he is Lord of heaven and earth, dwelleth not in temples made with hands; neither is worshipped with men's hands, as though he needed any thing, seeing he giveth to all life, and breath, and all things; and hath made of one blood all nations of men for to dwell on all the face of the earth, and hath determined the times before appointed, and the bounds of their habitation; that they should seek the Lord, if haply they might feel after him, and find him, though he be not far from every one of us.**
>
> **Acts 17:24-27**

Paul's message was aimed at the incompatibility of idols with the very nature of God. Next Paul reminds them that idolatry is incompatible with the nature of man:

> **For in him we live, and move and have our being; as certain also of your own poets have said, For we are also his offspring. Forasmuch then as we are the offspring of God, we ought not to think that the Godhead is like unto gold, or silver, or stone, graven by art and man's device.**
>
> **Acts 17:28,29**

To these know-it-alls, Paul now tightens down the screws and exposes their ignorance of God and His demands upon men:

> **And the times of this ignorance God winked at; but now commandeth all men every where to repent: because he hath appointed a day, in the which he will judge the world in righteousness by that man whom he hath ordained; whereof he hath given assurance unto all men, in that he hath raised him from the dead.**
>
> **Acts 17:30,31**

Paul was quite comprehensive in his presentation of the true God—the God of creation, the source and sustainer of all life, the God of all mankind, the omnipresent God, the omnipotent God, the God who is a Spirit, the God who enlightens our ignorance and who demands repentance because He is the judge of all.

The Hardness of Athens

The resurrection, of course, is at the heart of our Christian faith. Paul did not fail to seal his message with the fact of Jesus' resurrection. The resurrection of Jesus Christ is our guarantee. The gospel, however, usually does not have its greatest impact on those who are wise after the flesh. No great church was founded in Athens during the first two hundred years of Christianity; the gospel message first had to dislodge thirteen hundred years of human wisdom and idolatry!

But Paul's sermon was not in vain, by any means. A distinguished member of the Athenian court was converted, as well as one Damaris, "and others with them." (Acts 17:34.)

I think Paul's experience in Athens stuck with him for some time. Later he would write:

> **For it is written, I will destroy the wisdom of the wise, and will bring to nothing the understanding of the**

prudent. Where is the wise? where is the scribe? where is the disputer of this world? hath not God made foolish the wisdom of this world?

> The resurrection is at the heart of our Christian faith.

For after that in the wisdom of God the world by wisdom knew not God, it pleased God by the foolishness of preaching to save them that believe. For the Jews require a sign, and the Greeks seek after wisdom: but we preach Christ crucified, unto the Jews a stumblingblock, and unto the Greeks foolishness; but unto them which are called, both Jews and Greeks, Christ the power of God, and the wisdom of God.

1 Corinthians 1:19-24

Athens would eventually become a strong Christian center, but for now Paul would push on to the city whose very name became a synonym for licentiousness: Corinth. Here Paul would stay for one-and-a-half years and build a thriving, if somewhat immature, church. Rather than approach his listeners in Corinth from an intellectual viewpoint, Paul's preaching would be "in demonstration of the Spirit and of power" (1 Cor. 2:4).

Chapter 15

Corruption at Corinth

(Acts 18-21:17)

*L*eaving the intellectual snobbery of Athens, Paul traveled forty-six miles to preach the gospel in quite a different setting—a first-century navy town that eventually became a synonym for licentiousness! Corinth was the political capital of Greece during Paul's day. Sea routes and land routes came together at Corinth, making it a commercial and trade center between Italy and all of Asia.

The temple of Venus was located in Corinth with more than one thousand male and female prostitutes added to the city's blatant corruption. The city of 500,000 people was actually proud of their reputation for looseness, but Paul was certainly not one to be intimidated; he knew that the gospel is "the power of God unto salvation to every one that believeth" (Rom. 1:16).

At Corinth Paul met Aquila and Priscilla, who were tentmakers as was Paul. Aquila and Priscilla had been affected by the persecution against all Jews in Rome. The Jews were appalled by the idolatry of the Romans. The Romans, in turn, were jealous of the Jewish diligence in areas of commerce, education, and government. Around 51 A.D. Rome expelled all Jews. In the case of Aquila and Priscilla, God used this for His purposes by bringing them into contact with Paul.

Paul was a tentmaker by trade, but he was also building the "tabernacle" of the Lord at Corinth within the hearts of the people. Tent making enabled Paul to give himself to missionary work. According to his custom, Paul used the Jewish synagogue as his forum:

And he reasoned in the synagogue every sabbath, and persuaded the Jews and the Greeks.

Acts 18:4

The Jews couldn't argue against Paul's message, so they finally blasphemed and essentially forced Paul to declare, "Your blood be upon your own heads; I am clean: from henceforth I will go unto the Gentiles" (Acts 18:6).

However, Paul didn't go far from the synagogue! He found an open door in the house of Justus, whose house was actually attached to the synagogue. Imagine the anger of the Jews in that part of town when their own chief ruler, Crispus, believed Paul's message and received Jesus as the Christ!

All of Crispus's house were saved and baptized. Then the Lord gave Paul a vision, telling him that He had many people in the city of Corinth. The vision strengthened and encouraged Paul.

Corinth was a ripened harvest field. Paul had seen very little success in preaching the gospel in Athens, but in Corinth there were many hungry hearts. Here Paul entered into a different phase of his missionary ministry. Unlike his past work where he seemed to go at a fast pace from place to place in the next five years, he would be centered between two cities—Corinth on the European mainland and Ephesus in Asia.

When a new proconsul, Gallio, was appointed in Corinth, the Jews evidently thought it was the right time to accuse Paul before the town judgment seat. Their tactic didn't work. Gallio dismissed the matter and told the Jews to solve their differences among themselves.

Ministry at Ephesus

When the time finally came for Paul to leave Corinth, he took Aquila and Priscilla with him and headed off for Ephesus, a flourishing city in Asia Minor. Ephesus was an important commercial city and its chief pride was the temple of Diana, or Artemis, which was one of the seven wonders of the ancient world. Shrewd Greek traders engaged in business relating to the idolatrous worship and magical art connected with the temple.

Again, Paul went to the synagogue and lost no time in presenting Jesus to the Jews. He did not stay long in Ephesus at this time; he must have had great faith in Aquila and Priscilla to leave them in Ephesus after so little personal time there. Paul stopped briefly at Caesarea, saluted the church in Jerusalem, and finally returned to Antioch.

Paul shared with his home church the victories of the harvest. He probably did not stay more than three months at Antioch, the place from which the church had originally sent him forth. Paul's mind was always on the mission field. On his second missionary journey, Paul had established New Testament local churches at Philippi, Thessalonica, Berea, Athens, and Corinth. The epistles to these churches give us tremendous revelation truth of Christ.

Paul's Third Journey for Jesus

When Paul returned to Ephesus during his third missionary trip, he met other believers whose understanding of Christianity was limited. They knew of the baptism of John, but not of the baptism of the Holy Spirit. They had been baptized in water and evidently had received the Lord Jesus as their Savior. Paul laid hands on them, and they spoke with tongues and prophesied. (Acts 19:1-7.) They received the Holy Spirit, the Helper Jesus had promised.

Paul went back into the Ephesian synagogue and for three months taught the Word of God, emphasizing the kingdom of God. The response from the Jews was typical of past experiences:

> **But when divers were hardened, and believed not, but spake evil of that way before the multitude, he departed from them, and separated the disciples, disputing daily in the school of one Tyrannus.**
>
> **Acts 19:9**

Paul spent two years teaching the believers in Ephesus, and God validated his authority by performing special miracles:

> **And God wrought special miracles by the hands of Paul: so that from his body were brought unto the sick handkerchiefs or aprons, and the diseases departed from them, and the evil spirits went out of them.**
>
> **Acts 19:11,12**

The Holy Spirit can use all kinds of things to show God's grace and healing power. The "handkerchiefs or aprons" were points of contact and certainly nothing to be worshiped.

Revival at Ephesus

Acts 19:13 tells us of "vagabond" Jews who were exorcists. These men were identified as the seven sons of Sceva, who was probably a member of the local Jewish Sanhedrin. His sons claimed special knowledge in casting out demons. Accordingly, they began commanding an evil spirit to come out in the power of "Jesus whom Paul preacheth." The demons knew Jesus, but the demons didn't know Sceva's sons. Look what happened when they tried to invoke authority they didn't have:

> **And the man in whom the evil spirit was leaped on them, and overcame them, and prevailed against them, so that they fled out of that house naked and wounded.**
>
> **Acts 19:16**

Because of this incident, the name of the Lord Jesus was magnified, and people were stirred up to renounce any past involvement in the occult. All kinds of books of magic and charms and curios used for spells were burned. After two years in Ephesus, Paul planned to go into Macedonia and Achaia, and he sent some of his men ahead. Timothy was one of those men. When he had returned from Macedonia, he rejoined Paul at Corinth. Timothy seems to have run another errand for Paul to Corinth:

> **For this cause have I sent unto you Timotheus, who is my beloved son, and faithful in the Lord, who shall**

**bring you into remembrance of my ways which be in
Christ, as I teach every where in every church.**

1 Corinthians 4:17

During this time there was another riot, but it was not the
Jews who became stirred up—it was the Gentiles. As we've seen,
with Gentiles the problem was not doctrine; it was money. They
derived their wealth from making silver miniatures of the temple
of Diana. Diana of the Ephesians was an obscenity, a gross image
with licentious rites. She had been the ancient goddess of Asia
Minor called Artemis.

Some of the tradesmen were concerned that they were going to
become bankrupt if the number of Paul's converts kept increasing.
A terrible riot broke out, and it was difficult to argue with a mob
that was blinded with passion. Eventually the mob was dispersed
by the town clerk.

Touring Macedonia and Greece

After the uproar was over, Paul departed for Macedonia where
he visited churches in Philippi, Thessalonica, and Berea. From
there he traveled into Greece, visiting churches in Athens,
Corinth, and Cenchrea. It only took three months in Greece to stir
up opposition again from the Jews. Paul had a quick change of
plans when he learned that the Jews were lying in wait for him.
Leaving Philippi, Paul sailed to Troas where he preached and held
the Lord's Supper on Sunday:

**And upon the first day of the week, when the disci-
ples came together to break bread, Paul preached unto**

them, ready to depart on the morrow; and continued his speech until midnight.

Acts 20:7

Though the early Church kept the first day of the week, we also see them keeping the feasts of the Passover and Unleavened Bread. This was a transition period, coming from the old covenant into the fullness of the new covenant. The feast days had been so extremely important to the Jews, but Paul said:

Blotting out the handwriting of ordinances that was against us, which was contrary to us, and took it out of the way, nailing it to his cross; and having spoiled principalities and powers, he made a shew of them openly, triumphing over them in it. Let no man therefore judge you in meat, or in drink, or in respect of an holyday, or of the new moon, or of the sabbath days.

Colossians 2:14-16

The true Sabbath is the rest in Christ and the baptism of the Holy Spirit:

There remaineth therefore a rest to the people of God.

Hebrews 4:9

For precept must be upon precept, precept upon precept; line upon line, line upon line; here a little, and there a little: for with stammering lips and another tongue will he speak to this people. To whom he said, This is the rest wherewith ye may cause the weary to rest; and this is the refreshing: yet they would not hear.

Isaiah 28:10-12

The old sabbath, the seventh day of the week, was a sign for the *nation of Israel:*

> **Wherefore the children of Israel shall keep the sabbath, to observe the sabbath throughout their generations, for a perpetual covenant. It is a sign between me and the children of Israel for ever: for in six days the Lord made heaven and earth, and on the seventh day he rested, and was refreshed.**
>
> **Exodus 31:16,17**

The new covenant had a new day on which to worship. The early Church broke bread on the first day of the week:

> **And upon the first day of the week, when the disciples came together to break bread, Paul preached unto them, ready to depart on the morrow; and continued his speech until midnight.**
>
> **Acts 20:7**

They laid aside their collections on the first day of the week:

> **Upon the first day of the week let every one of you lay by him in store, as God hath prospered him, that there be no gatherings when I come.**
>
> **1 Corinthians 16:2**

Jesus arose on the first day of the week, and the Holy Spirit was poured out at Pentecost on the first day of the week. It's not hard to see why the Jews hated Paul; he preached about, wrote about, and personally celebrated a "new Sabbath" that would have infuriated the followers of Moses.

So now at Troas, Paul again broke bread with the disciples and preached a lengthy sermon. Paul continued his preaching until very late. The Upper Room was three stories up, and a sleepy young man fell out of the window to his death, but by the power of the Holy Spirit, Paul operated in the gift of miracles, and the young man was raised from the dead!

Ministry on the Way to Jerusalem

Later, Paul walked the twenty miles to Assos while the others in his party went by ship. Perhaps he wanted the time alone.

After a number of quick stops along the coast, Paul arrived at Miletus, where he sent a messenger to Ephesus to call a meeting of the elders of that church. They walked the thirty miles from Ephesus to Miletus to hear a final message from the great apostle. Paul charged them, "Feed the church of God, which he hath purchased with his own blood" (Acts 20:28).

Chapter 21 begins Paul's ministry at Tyre. This is an ancient Phoenician city, but it had a church there that was established after the persecution of Stephen. (Acts 11:19.)

As we discussed earlier, Paul was warned of the danger awaiting him in Jerusalem, but that did not deter him from following God's leading in his spirit. From Tyre, Paul and his group went to Ptolemais and then on to Caesarea, where they lodged with Philip the evangelist, one of the seven original deacons of the Jerusalem church. He took the gospel to the Samaritans and was used mightily.

Agabus gave Paul his last warning about the suffering awaiting him if he went to Jerusalem. (Acts 21:11.) Paul knew in his spirit that bonds and imprisonment were awaiting him. He had already proclaimed:

> **And now, behold I go bound in the spirit unto Jerusalem, not knowing the things that shall befall me there: save that the Holy Ghost witnesseth in every city, saying that bonds and afflictions abide me.**
>
> **Acts 20:22-24**

Paul also knew in his spirit that he would go to Rome:

> **After these things were ended, Paul purposed in the spirit, when he had passed through Macedonia and Achaia, to go to Jerusalem, saying, After I have been there, I must also see Rome.**
>
> **Acts 19:21**

Paul knew that he was to go, and he also knew the afflictions that awaited him. He knew God's will, even though others would not accept his witness. After Agabus's final warning, he cried:

> **What mean ye to weep and to break mine heart? for I am ready not to be bound only, but also to die at Jerusalem for the name of the Lord Jesus.**
>
> **Acts 21:13**

When the brethren could not persuade Paul to give up his plans, they simply said to him, "The will of the Lord be done" (v. 14). Paul knew the will of God, and he purposed in his heart to obey the Lord's leading.

As Paul made his journey to Jerusalem, he went in the Spirit. (Acts 20:22.) He wanted to go to Rome and then to Spain. He went to Rome in chains as a prisoner, but more than that, he was a prisoner of the Holy Spirit. The Holy Spirit moved upon the people to warn him about going to Jerusalem. (Acts 21:4,10,11.) If Paul had gone to Jerusalem without all these warnings, the

Judaizers would have taken his arrest as a judgment of God. This would have certainly brought great confusion to the Church. But the Spirit bore witness to Paul and the gospel he preached through this Spirit manifestation.

The Spirit is the Protector and unquestionably the Guide of the Church. The book of Acts shows us that all believers are to be baptized in the Holy Spirit, empowered by Him, taught to be His disciples, and directed and constrained by Him. Every believer is to be a witness by the power of the Holy Spirit.

It was sixty-five miles from Caesarea to Jerusalem. When Paul arrived in Jerusalem, the brethren there gladly received him. Their joy would be short-lived; in a little over a week, Paul would be beaten by the Jews and arrested by the Gentiles.

It was just the beginning of his long trip to Rome and the suffering that the Holy Spirit had shown him was to come.

Chapter 16

Judgment Upon the Judges

(Acts 24-26)

Wouldn't you be excited if you knew that God wanted you to speak before kings and rulers? If you weren't careful, it might be easy to become a bit boastful and proud! God told Ananias that Paul would bear His name before "Gentiles, and kings, and the children of Israel" (Acts 9:15). Little did Paul know at that time what the conditions would be when he finally stood before the rulers of his day as a prisoner of the state. No room for any pride there!

Chapters 24-26 of Acts give a good look at the fulfillment of this prophecy in Paul's life. We see the apostle bearing the name of Jesus before governors Felix and Festus and before King Agrippa. Sadly, there is no record of their receiving Paul's witness.

For their case against Paul, the Jews—led by the high priest Ananias—brought in a smooth talker named Tertullus. They probably thought they had their case all wrapped up. Tertullus was a flatterer and a liar. Let's look at the charges they brought against Paul (Acts 24:5,6):

1. He was a pestilent fellow.

2. He was a mover of sedition.

3. He was the ringleader of the sect of the Nazarenes.

4. He profaned the temple.

Evidently the Jews had decided not to call Paul a "Christian" but rather a "Nazarene." The Galilean town of Nazareth was a despised town.

The following is Paul's defense before the governor, Felix, against the false accusations (v. 10-21):

1. Paul had not been found in the temple "disputing with any man."

2. Paul had not been "raising up the people" in the synagogues or anywhere in the city.

3. The Jews could present no proof for any of their charges.

4. Paul brought in his witness about the Lord Jesus Christ.

5. Paul told of his hope of the resurrection of the just.

6. Paul testified that he went to Jerusalem, taking alms and offerings to the people.

7. Paul said he was fulfilling a vow of purification; it was Jews from Asia who caused the problem.

8. There were no Asian Jews there to give any evidence.

9. The only disruption caused by Paul was when he alleged that he was on trial before the Sanhedrin because of his belief in the resurrection.

It appears that Felix knew more than the Jews about the sect of the Nazarene. He deferred Paul's case until the chief captain Lysias came down from Jerusalem to give further evidence. Paul was kept in custody, but his friends were allowed to visit him. Paul was given every consideration as a Roman citizen. Of course, Felix knew that Ananias and his crowd were scoundrels and liars.

Oddly, no Christians from Jerusalem came to Paul's aid while in custody there, nor did they help him with his testimony or stand with him. Days later, Felix brought his wife, Drusilla, to hear Paul. Drusilla was a Jewess. She was the youngest daughter of Herod Agrippa I. This is the Herod who murdered James and would have murdered Peter. (Acts 12:1-3.)

Paul, as he sat before Drusilla and Felix, strongly preached righteousness, temperance, and the judgment to come. The Holy Spirit dealt with Felix, for Paul's words were like sharp swords into Felix's conscience. Felix trembled, he was terrified, he was convicted, but it looks like cash was on his mind more than Christ. Acts 24:26 tells us that Felix was hoping for a bribe from Paul for his freedom.

How sad! Though Paul preached of righteousness, Felix wanted Paul to be *unrighteous* in offering a bribe.

Festus Hears the Gospel

Two years went by, after which there was a civil war between the Jews and Gentiles at Caesarea. Felix gathered troops and ended the war, using great violence against the Jews. Authorities in Rome demanded an account of his behavior. In the meantime, Paul was handed over to Procius Festus, the new procurator.

The new governor couldn't have cared less about Paul. He merely wanted favor with the Jews under his charge, so he left Paul imprisoned. Festus went to Jerusalem and faced the Sanhedrin. The Jews were very clever, and Festus certainly wanted to get along with them.

The Jewish leadership put much pressure on Festus to get Paul released from Caesarea and back to trial in Jerusalem, but God holds the hearts of men in His hands, and Festus didn't give in to the Jews' request. God overrode the Jewish leadership.

After ten days Festus returned to Caesarea and brought Paul before the judgment seat. It must have been a terribly frustrating time for Paul—to have to appear before Festus when he had already appeared before Felix, whom knew he was innocent. Festus knew less about Jewish law, and it would be even more difficult for Paul to defend himself, but Paul's faith was not in man's knowledge; it was in God.

The Jews came down with their same complaints. Then they added some charges against Paul concerning Caesar. Luke summarizes Paul's defense:

> **While he answered for himself, Neither against the law of the Jews, neither against the temple, nor yet against Caesar, have I offended any thing at all.**
>
> **Acts 25:8**

Paul took a strong stand for Christian obedience to governing powers. Earlier he had written to the Christians living in Rome:

Let every soul be subject unto the higher powers. For there is no power but of God: the powers that be are ordained of God. Whosoever therefore resisteth the power, resisteth the ordinance of God: and they that resist shall receive to themselves damnation. For rulers are not a terror to good works, but to the evil. Wilt thou then not be afraid of the power? do that which is good, and thou shalt have praise of the same.

Romans 13:1-3

Festus asked Paul whether he would like to go to Jerusalem to be judged. Paul, knowing that he must bear witness in Rome, exercised his Roman citizenship and appealed to Caesar. Festus conferred with his private council and agreed to send Paul to Rome.

Agrippa Hears the Gospel

In the meantime King Agrippa and his wife came to Caesarea to pay their respects to the new governor. Agrippa was well acquainted with Jewish law, and after some days Festus spoke to him about Paul's case.

Paul's chains were God's vehicles to bring the gospel to kings. Paul spoke with respect to leadership all the way through his trials. At each divine opportunity before the rulers, Paul gave his testimony. We never read of any bitterness toward God in Paul's testimonies; like many prophets before him, Paul was never disobedient to his vision.

Paul's Altar Call

When Paul was given the chance to speak before Festus and Agrippa, he was not just reciting a set of facts but preaching the gospel. Paul's message included a call for repentance and good works:

> **...that they should repent and turn to God, and do works meet for repentance.**
>
> **Acts 26:20**

Paul's message was nothing more than what Moses and all the Jewish prophets had declared:

> **That Christ should suffer, and that he should be the first that should rise from the dead, and should shew light unto the people, and to the Gentiles.**
>
> **Acts 26:23**

Festus declared Paul mad. Of course, others had said the same thing about Jesus. Festus could see only one world; Paul was in touch with both worlds—the present world and the world to come. Festus could not believe in the resurrection, though over five hundred credible witnesses had seen Jesus after His death.

However, Agrippa knew Paul's message was true. Paul appealed to Agrippa and sought a decision from this king. In response, Paul heard some of the saddest words recorded in the Bible:

> **Almost thou persuadest me to be a Christian.**
>
> **Acts 26:28**

Had Agrippa become a Christian, he would have been sneered at and looked down upon. It would have cost him something, but denying Christ cost Agrippa everything—it cost him his very soul.

Now, Paul's appeal to Caesar was already on record. Agrippa wanted to free him, but God wanted Paul in Rome. Thus he would stand before the deranged son of Agrippina, the fifth emperor of the Roman Empire—Caesar Nero.

But first Paul would survive a lethal storm at sea and a deadly snakebite!

Chapter 17

The Holy Spirit, Your Deliverer!

(*Acts 27, 28*)

oes it sometimes feel as if circumstances are against what you know to be the will of God? What do you do at times like those? Do you give up? Forget the Spirit's leading and change your mind about God's will for you? Or do you stand on the Word of God and use your stumbling blocks as stepping stones to higher ground?

The Holy Spirit's anointing is able to deliver people from sin's bondage and Satan's grasp, and release them into the wealth and freedom of God's kingdom. Isaiah prophesied a time when burdens would be lifted and bondage would be broken because of the anointing:

> **And it shall come to pass in that day, that his burden shall be taken away from off thy shoulder, and his yoke from off thy neck, and the yoke shall be destroyed because of the anointing**
>
> Isaiah 10:27

I believe that the Holy Spirit included the events in these last two chapters of Acts to encourage your faith and to assure you of God's presence in every circumstance of life.

Paul must have felt the same way. But despite all circumstances to the contrary, he knew that his destiny lay in Rome. Each obstacle—stoning, trials, and imprisonment—only made Paul more determined to reach his goal. Acts 19:21 tells us Paul had "purposed in the spirit" to go to Rome.

Paul's confidence about reaching his final destination was in God's Word and God's leading in his spirit and trust in the Holy Spirit to deliver him. What's your "Rome"? What goal or destination are you presently working toward? I believe that the Holy Spirit included the events in these last two chapters of Acts to encourage your faith and to assure you of God's presence in every circumstance of life.

Paul's Faithful Friends

Luke was with Paul during his stay in Caesarea, but he kept himself out of the narrative until the first verse of chapter 27:

And when it was determined that we should sail into Italy, they delivered Paul and certain other prisoners unto one named Julius, a centurion of Augustus' band.

Acts 27:1

Paul's other traveling companion was Aristarchus, who was first mentioned on Paul's trip to Thessalonica. (Acts 19:29.)

These men went with Paul to Jerusalem with the money given from the Gentile churches, but it's speculated that in order to accompany Paul to Rome, Luke and Aristarchus had to go as Paul's slaves. What love they had for Paul!

In time, they sailed "under Cyprus" and dropped anchor at Myra in the southern part of Asia Minor, where they changed ships.

Egypt shipped much grain to the Roman Empire, and these grain ships were large. The centurion asked for space on the ship and transferred the prisoners. It took many days to sail from Myra to Fair Havens because they faced contrary winds.

At this point Paul spoke up and issued a warning by the direction of the Holy Spirit of what was to come if they continued sailing. Acts 27:9 tells us, "Sailing was now dangerous, because the fast was now already past." This refers to Yom Kippur, the Day of Atonement, which is celebrated on the tenth day of the seventh month. (Lev. 23:27.) This would be around the first of October. The most dangerous times to sail were mid-September to mid-November. However, Paul's warnings were rejected; the centurion in charge trusted in the word of man more than in the Word of God:

Nevertheless the centurion believed the master and the owner of the ship, more than those things which were spoken by Paul.

Acts 27:11

They set sail with a deceptively smooth south wind, which soon changed to a violent wind.

A Storm at Sea

The sailors were afraid that they might be driven into some of the sandbars around the coast; the storm, however, took them out into the deep waters. The first day was a dreadful one. The next day, they had to throw out the cargo. On the third day they had to throw out the tackling of the ship—the sail and all the ship's furnishings. What else could they do but throw themselves into the hands of God? God was permitting them to come to a place where they would believe and submit to His Word.

I am sure that by this time the centurion was sorry he had believed the owner of the ship rather than Paul, but because of Paul's faith, an angel of God, a ministering spirit, came to minister to Paul in the storm. He later told the crew:

For there stood by me this night the angel of God, whose I am, and whom I serve, saying, Fear not, Paul; thou must be brought before Caesar: and, lo, God hath given thee all them that sail with thee.

Acts 27:23,24

Unsaved people certainly are blessed by the presence of saved people! The passengers and prisoners were blessed because of

Paul. Today the whole world is blessed because of the presence of the Church.

Paul told the ship's crew that they would be cast upon an island without any loss of life. On the fourteenth night about midnight the sailors knew they were near land. The fourteenth night could symbolize Passover, according to Exodus 12:1-6 and 11:4. According to Matthew 25:1-13 and Mark 13:35, the hour of midnight may symbolize the end of the age. The spiritual lesson here is that full salvation comes through the Passover Lamb upon His Second Coming.

Paul encouraged all 276 persons aboard the ship to take bread and give thanks, that assuredly they would make it safely to shore because no matter what they went through, God had promised Paul that he would stand before Caesar. God wanted Caesar, one of the most wretched men who ever walked this earth, to hear the gospel—and to hear it from Paul's lips.

In the meantime, the storm was driving the ship to shore; the ship would soon run aground. The sailors decided that they would leave the ship in a small boat and leave the prisoners to their deaths aboard the ship, but Paul saw through what they were trying to do and told the centurion that all needed to stay aboard for all to be saved. By this time the centurion had learned to listen to Paul, and the skiff was cut loose without anyone's leaving the ship.

When they finally ran aground, the soldiers wanted to kill the prisoners. This seems cruel, but Roman code dictated that every Roman soldier was personally responsible for his prisoner. If that prisoner escaped, the soldier had to give his own life in forfeit.

The soldiers were afraid; but again, the centurion, who was Paul's friend by now, was determined to save him. He commanded that all prisoners be allowed to swim to shore. When they did, all of those aboard the ship made it safely ashore to the island of Melita.

The word *Melita* is a Canaanite word that means "refuge." Today the island is called Malta. The islanders were very gracious in providing a fire to warm the shipwrecked travelers.

The devil had tried his best to drown Paul at sea, but Paul had a divine appointment in Rome. When drowning didn't work, the devil tried to eliminate Paul through a snakebite! While Paul helped gather wood for a fire, a snake bit him. Paul shook the snake into the fire, and the fact that he didn't die was a great sign to the islanders.

Publius, the head of the island, lodged Paul and his group for three days. When the father of Publius became sick, Paul laid hands on him, and God healed him. News of the miracle spread, and others from the island brought the sick to Paul:

So when this was done, others also, which had diseases in the island, came, and were healed.

Acts 28:9

What a marvelous account of the gifts of the Holy Spirit in action! Paul used the gift of healing to bless all who were sick on the island. Ministering healing to their bodies opened the way for ministry to their spirits. Never before in the book of Acts had Paul been so welcomed and honored as he was here. Melita was truly a refuge for Paul.

Today the Holy Spirit, our Comforter, offers us a place of refuge for believers and unbelievers. For Christians it is a place of refuge from the daily contamination that results from being in the world but not of it. Whenever you feel "out of it," depressed, lonely, or sick, *run* to church and take refuge in the presence of God and the fellowship of other Spirit-filled saints!

For unbelievers, the church is the *only* refuge from the coming judgment. You and I can lead others to this refuge, and like Paul, God has given us the authority to lay hands on the sick and to see them recover:

> **And these signs shall follow them that believe; In my name shall they cast out devils; they shall speak with new tongues; they shall take up serpents; and if they drink any deadly thing, it shall not hurt them; they shall lay hands on the sick, and they shall recover.**
>
> **Mark 16:17,18**

Whenever you feel "out of it," depressed, lonely, or sick, *run* to church and take refuge in the presence of God and the fellowship of other Spirit-filled saints!

Remember that the working of the supernatural is not the Holy Spirit's way of making you a "big name." The supernatural lifts up the name of Jesus and provides an inroad for the preaching of the gospel. Step out in faith to those around you, and God will meet their *physical* and *spiritual* needs through you.

Rome at Last

After three months, Paul and his group set sail and at long last came to Rome. Immediately Paul began to witness to the Jews living there. Jesus had told him to go to the uttermost parts of the earth, and Paul was about his Master's business.

> And when they had appointed him a day, there came many to him into his lodging; to whom he expounded and testified the kingdom of God, persuading them concerning Jesus, both out of the law of Moses, and out of the prophets, from morning till evening.
>
> Acts 28:23

The reaction of the Jews was the same everywhere Paul had traveled:

> And some believed the things, which were spoken, and some believed not.
>
> Acts 28:24

Paul loved the Jews, and their rejection of his good news must have saddened him. Finally he spoke to them, quoting from the prophet Isaiah:

> Well spake the Holy Ghost by Esaias the prophet unto our fathers, saying, Go unto this people, and say, Hearing ye shall hear, and shall not understand; and seeing ye shall see, and not perceive: for the heart of this people is waxed gross, and their ears are dull of hearing, and their eyes have they closed; lest they should see with their eyes, and hear with their ears, and understand with their heart, and should be converted, and I should heal them.
>
> Acts 28:25-27

This prophecy is quoted five other times in the New Testament. (Matt. 13:13; Mark 4:12; Luke 8:10; John 12:40; Rom. 11:8.) Surely the Holy Spirit thinks its message is important.

Paul quoted the prophecy for the last time. This was the closing of the door—the day of the Jews' privilege was over. In a few short years, the temple would be demolished and the Romans would tread down Jerusalem.

Paul's Prison Ministry

During Paul's first period of imprisonment, he wrote the books of the Bible that we now call Philippians, Ephesians, Colossians, and Philemon. Paul's incarceration was not wasted time, but time that would bless the Body of Christ forever. He won many to Christ; he even had contacts in Caesar's household:

> **All the saints salute you, chiefly they that are of Caesar's household.**
>
> Philippians 4:22

Paul might have been locked up, but he never shut up! Although he was imprisoned for a number of years, Paul was perhaps one of the greatest travelers of his day. He visited many lands and saw many new scenes in different countries, but he was blind to everything save Jesus and the leading of His Holy Spirit.

From the time he met the Lord Jesus on the road to Damascus, he was blinded by the vision of Christ's great glory and could no longer see anything but Jesus nor tell of anything but His gospel.

Jesus wants you and me to speak up boldly and to walk in the same glory and miracle-working power as Paul and the early Church did. He has given us the

He has given us the power of the Holy Spirit, and if we will believe as the early Church believed, then we will act as the early Church acted; then we will experience the same power and anointing as they did.

power of the Holy Spirit, and if we will believe as the early Church believed, then we will act as the early Church acted; then we will experience the same power and anointing as they did.

Jesus is coming back for a glorious Church; our prayer should be the same prayer for power spoken by the apostles in Acts 4:29-30: "Lord...grant unto thy servants, that with all boldness they may speak thy word...and that signs and wonders may be done in the name of thy holy child Jesus."

Likewise, after such a prayer, we will experience what those praying disciples experienced: "The place was shaken where they were assembled together; and they were all filled with the Holy Ghost, and they spake the word of God with boldness" (v. 31).

Chapter 18

The Holy
Spirit Today

We've seen the God-ordained role of the Holy Spirit, how He operated in the Old Testament, and the marvelous works He performed through the early Church in the book of Acts. What is His role today?

In the contemporary Church, we need to prepare ourselves to receive the manifest presence of God through the outpouring of the Holy Spirit. The fire that was poured out on the Day of Pentecost continues to burn today.

There is something about His manifested presence that changes you more than anything else. When Jacob wrestled with the angel, I believe he was actually wrestling with the manifested presence of

God. God touched Jacob that day, and he was never the same again; he became Israel. (Gen. 32:24-30.)

And when Saul, the persecutor of the Church, was on the road to Damascus, Jesus manifested Himself to him in a vision and said, "Saul, Saul, why persecutest thou me?" (Acts 9:4).

Saul cried out, "Who are you?" And Jesus answered, "I am Jesus whom thou persecutest" (v.5).

From that moment of experiencing the manifested presence of God, Saul would never be the same. As we've seen, he went on to become Paul, the great apostle who wrote a third of the New Testament.

In Exodus 32, we read that the Israelites made a golden calf and worshiped it. This was after God had manifested His presence to them in a cloud by day and a pillar of fire by night. The Israelites knew His presence, they felt His presence, they saw His presence. When they disobeyed anyway, God told Moses that He would withdraw His presence from the people.

We must have God's manifested presence in the Church today, and that requires preparation.

Moses beseeched God to give the people a second chance. He told God, "We must have Your manifested presence!" (Ex. 33:15.)

Likewise, we must have God's manifested presence in the Church today, and that requires preparation. Pray, sanctify yourself, and set aside anything God has spoken to you about.

When Moses did this, God answered, "My presence shall go with thee, and I will give thee rest" (Ex. 33:14). God will say the same thing to the Church today if we will only appreciate and esteem His presence.

God wants to bring Holy Spirit revival to the Body of Christ, but it takes preparation on our part. God thinks the process of preparation is just as important as the finished product. If we can allow the Holy Spirit to work in us the way He wants to work and be surrendered to Him the way He wants us to surrender, then He can produce what He wants in us.

We need the manifested presence of God. We need it in our daily lives—at home, at church, on the job, in our families, and with our spouses. We need to be able to touch Him and know Him in a personal way, and God has given us access through our Helper, the Holy Spirit.

We need to be able to touch Him and know Him in a personal way, and God has given us access through our Helper, the Holy Spirit.

Genesis 28:16 says, "And Jacob awaked out of his sleep, and he said, Surely the Lord is in this place; and I knew it not." Clearly, we need to cultivate an awareness of His presence in us through the Holy Spirit, and praising God cultivates this awareness.

Learn to live in an atmosphere of praise, because according to Psalm 22:3, God inhabits the praises of His people.

I had something unusual happen to me as a result of cultivating an awareness of the Lord's presence. I came home from an overseas trip and traveled to Texas the next day for a series of meetings. It actually was a "Psalms encounter"; the glory of God came down, and I never really even got to teach!

In the meantime, I was adjusting to a 16-hour time change and jet lag. It was almost as though, while spending time in the presence of God, my body didn't need any sleep for almost four days. I felt as if I were living in a capsule of the presence of God.

Wonderful things were happening in the meetings. People were saved and filled with the Spirit. By the second day, I knew something was cooking. Have you ever felt like God was cooking up something? I could feel it.

I began teaching on Psalms, and people began crying! When the altar call was over and the service dismissed, nobody left. People stayed and just basked in the presence of God. Several people reported that they had visions of what God was doing in their lives.

That night I preached the third part of Psalms. All at once, people on one side of the church began fanning themselves. I thought, *It must be hot on that side of the building,* but pretty soon, they started laughing. I thought, *What's so funny?* And then a man fell into the aisle. At that point, my teaching was over! People in the back started laughing in the Spirit, and the entire front row fell on the floor, drunk in the Spirit.

That was the manifested presence of God. Sometimes we desperately need visitations such as those, because our problems can be so tremendous and we can face such demonic attacks, but when you begin to experience God's presence, it changes you; you won't ever be the same.

Why is it so important to cultivate God's presence through the Holy Spirit? Let's look at what happens in His presence.

First, God says in His presence is fullness of joy. (Ps. 16:11.) You can be wrestling under problems and fighting all kinds of situations—you can be sick, losing all your finances, struggling in your marriage, or struggling with your kids—but when the joy of the Lord hits you, all those things go out the window, and then you can even *laugh* in His presence!

Second, in God's presence is also the discerning of sin. Genesis 3:8 says of Adam and Eve:

They heard the voice of the Lord God walking in the garden in the cool of the day: and Adam and his wife hid themselves from the presence of the Lord God amongst the trees of the garden.

They hid themselves from God's presence because they had sinned and God's presence brought heavy conviction upon them.

That's why, during our Psalms encounter in Texas, many people were laughing *and* crying. Some were full of the joy of the Lord, but others were repenting of sins. God's presence through the Holy Spirit identifies sin.

I think of Cain, Adam and Eve's son. Genesis 4:16 says:

And Cain went out from the presence of the Lord, and dwelt in the land of Nod, on the east of Eden.

Rather than repent for the sin of murdering his brother, Abel, Cain left the presence of God. How sad! That's why when God deals with you about sin, it's so important not to close your eyes and pretend it's not there. You run the danger of missing out on the blessings of God's manifested presence in your life.

Third, the manifest presence of God turns back your enemies. God's presence takes care of a lot of enemies we can never take care of ourselves. We may do all kinds of things, but those enemies just hang on; however, if we will let God's presence fill our circumstances, He'll take care of our enemies. The psalmist said, "When mine enemies are turned back, they shall fall and perish at thy presence" (Ps. 9:3).

The manifest presence of God turns back your enemies.

Once when we were ministering in Uganda, someone told us about an evangelist there. One night a group of rebels broke into his house while the evangelist and his family were sitting at the dinner table. The rebels said, "We want your money."

The evangelist told the rebels where to find the money. When they came back, one of the rebels said, "That's not enough. I'm going to kill you if you don't tell me where the money is." And he put a pistol to his head.

The evangelist protested, "I don't have any more money!"

"Well, then I'm going to kill you," the gunman said. He pulled the trigger.

The gun didn't go off. He pulled it again and nothing happened. A third time he pulled it. When it *still* didn't go off, the gunman said, "What are you anyway—what do you do?"

"I'm a Christian evangelist," the man answered.

Now, we wondered how his wife and children responded to all this, but apparently the evangelist had only commented, "God's manifested presence was so rich to us there—all we could think about was His presence." Let me tell you, God knows how to manifest His presence and take care of your enemies!

I heard about another time in which a Buddhist man came to a church service. A friend had invited him to go. He was sitting in the service thinking, *This is a lot of junk. I don't believe in this.*

He was about to get up and walk out, and he put his hand down on the pew in front of him, but when he did, it stuck! So he pulled and pulled and pulled, and when he finally managed to jerk his hand away, he hit his head on the back of the pew. It stuck!

When he finally got his head up, it hit his knee, and when his head hit his knee, it stuck again!

He pulled and pulled and finally got his head up from his knee—only to fall back on the floor. His head stuck again. While he was trying to get his head off the floor, he had a vision of Jesus Christ. Needless to say, he got saved!

The manifest presence of God takes care of the enemies of the gospel—*and* causes sinners to get saved!

God's presence also gives direction. Psalm 17:2 says, "Let my sentence come forth from thy presence; let thine eyes behold the things that are equal."

Sometimes we try to do things on our own, but we see how far that goes—not very far. People have asked me before, "Aren't you afraid to go overseas?" But I'm not, even when I go alone. Why would I be afraid? If God directs me to do something, He's big enough to take care of me. I've traveled in the ministry for years, and God has always taken care of me because I have His direction.

Fourth, when you have God's presence with you, you have rest. Exodus 33:14 says, "My presence will go with thee, and I will give thee rest."

There is something about the presence of God. Everything can be falling apart, but you feel like you're on a vacation because you're so wrapped up in His presence.

I think the reason many Christians worry, fuss, and fret so much is that we are not experiencing the power of God as we should. There have been times when I've awakened in the night because of some fearful situation, but then I've experienced God's presence and gotten such a rest in the midst of the circumstances.

Fifth, we are also saved from affliction in the presence of God.

In all their affliction he was afflicted, and the angel of his presence saved them: in his love and in his pity he redeemed them; and he bare them, and carried them all the days of old.

Isaiah 63:9

Maybe you're thinking, *I really am afflicted. I'm having a terrible crisis.* This Scripture says His presence is in your affliction, and because of His presence, you can come through it all with a wonderful miracle.

Sixth, His manifested presence is so important to cultivate because that is what we will experience for eternity. Jude 24 and 25 says:

Now unto him that is able to keep you from falling, and to present you faultless before the presence of his glory with exceeding joy...be glory and majesty, dominion and power.

So those times of the Holy Spirit's touching and refreshing us, giving us rest and direction, convicting us of sin, and giving us joy—all are just a taste of what we'll experience throughout eternity.

Don't miss what God has for you in His presence through the Holy Spirit's indwelling you! Say, "God, I must have a manifestation of Your presence. I can't go on without knowing Your touch. However You want to do so, I'm available." It's so important to have God's presence in our lives through the Holy Spirit. God wants to have encounters with us just like the Psalms encounters I had in my seminar.

It's scriptural. When Paul had an encounter with God at Damascus, for example, he didn't resist the Holy Spirit; he went down to the floor!

Now, encounters with the Holy Spirit can come in different ways. Some are not as dramatic as others. Paul had another encounter on his second missionary journey. He didn't know which direction to go, and he kept trying to go the Asian route, but he just couldn't get a witness in his heart.

Have you ever tried to do something and you couldn't quite get the mind of God? You think, *Well, God, I'm trying to hear You, but would You speak up?*

So one night Paul had a dream, and in it, a man said, "Come to Macedonia." And Paul shifted his plans because he had an encounter with the Holy Spirit.

In this second encounter, he didn't have a vision, he didn't see a light, he wasn't slapped to the ground or blinded for a few days. He just had a dream. (Acts 16:6-10.)

You can have an encounter with the Holy Spirit in laughter, in weeping, in prayer, while reading your Bible. Encounters come in different ways. When you begin to have encounters, usually it means God's taking you to another level. It means there's something He wants you to do. He doesn't give them to you for a little tickle and a thrill. He gives you encounters to take you into ministry—to fill you and spill you!

> **He gives you encounters to take you into ministry—to fill you and spill you!**

Be Filled and Spilled!

When the Lord fills us with His Spirit, He fills us with a purpose. We saw this clearly in the book of Acts—the wonderful miracles working through people after the mighty filling of the Holy Spirit.

Say you put a dry sponge in water. What happens? It soaks up the water. That's the way it is with the filling of the Holy Spirit—we "soak up" the Spirit.

But when the sponge is all filled up and won't soak up any more water, then what happens? It drips. Now, there are a lot of people who are filled with the Spirit who never let the anointing spill out of them; they just drip.

On the other hand, you can squeeze the sponge and release the water, spilling it. God doesn't want drips; He wants spills!

Look at Peter, for example. As we've seen, the disciple who had denied Christ stood up on the Day of Pentecost full of the Holy Spirit and preached to the multitude. Three thousand were saved! (Acts 2.)

There's something else interesting about this: Peter was initially filled with the Spirit according to Acts 2:4—the outpouring of the Holy Spirit. Acts 4:8 says, "Then Peter, filled with the Holy Ghost...." And verse 31 says, "And they were all filled with the Holy Ghost."

Notice that these fillings happen after the initial outpouring. You see, *there are more fillings!* When you get spilled, you have to get filled again.

Part of the purpose of the infilling presence of the Holy Spirit is for God to use us for ministry.

What Are You Clothed In?

Just how does God use us for ministry? I want us to look at Luke 24:49. It's very powerful and will help you receive what God wants you to have—something very, very special: power.

And, behold, I send the promise of my Father upon you: but tarry ye in the city of Jerusalem, until ye be endued with power from on high.

This is Jesus' saying to the disciples, "Wait on Me. Don't do anything else—because you really can't without the power of the Holy Spirit." He told them they would be "endued with power."

Now, *endued* means "clothed."[1] Jesus wants to *clothe* us in the Spirit. In the natural, what you put on affects what you look like. Likewise, spiritually when we are clothed in the Holy Spirit, we begin to look like—and act like—the Holy Spirit.

I talked once to a pastor's wife who was heading up a ministry to teenagers. She felt led of the Spirit to take the team over to a discotheque in the heart of the city, where most of the town's teenagers danced, drank, and used drugs. She and her team were going to hand out tracts and witness as the teenagers came and went. From midnight until three in the morning they did this.

Finally, the owner of the discotheque came out and began to harass this woman. "You shouldn't be out here doing this," he said. "You're hurting our business."

She answered, "This street doesn't belong to you; the sidewalk belongs to the city. I have as much access to this sidewalk as you do, and I'm going to stay."

He shrugged and said, "You may be very sorry if you stay."

That pastor's wife said later, "I was so bold, I knew I'd never be sorry. God called me there, and I knew I'd be all right. So I told the owner, 'Well, I'll be here. As long as God tells me to be here, I'm going to be here!'"

After several nights of this, the weary owner finally said, "You know, you think you're such hot stuff. If you've got so much to say, why don't you come inside and say it!"

In her heart, the Holy Spirit whispered, *Not tonight.*

"Why not, Lord?" she asked.

Because they only have a little band tonight, which means there's only a little crowd. The big band is next week; then the house will be full. Call him on it.

So she told the owner, "You just want me to come inside when there's a little crowd. No way! The only way I'll come in is when there is a big band in there and the room is filled. That's next Wednesday night."

The owner didn't know what to do. So he let her speak.

That Wednesday night the pastor's wife went into the club. It was jam-packed. She got up on stage in the midst of the lights and the noise and the crowd and said, "I have ten minutes, and I'm going to tell it to you straight. You know Jesus loves you, and some of you know better than to be in here. You're backslidden and cold toward God, but right now I want you to have the guts to stand up and walk out of here with me."

Half of the crowd stood up and walked out with her! Hallelujah! Now how was she able to do that? She was clothed with the Spirit, with power, with the anointing.

Now, we may make the mistake of thinking that being clothed in the Spirit is a process. It's not a process; it's an immediate experience.

When the disciples were baptized on the Day of Pentecost, it wasn't a process! And there's no question that they were indeed clothed, because they went out afterward and began healing the sick, raising the dead, and setting at liberty those who were captive.

But sometimes we don't think we're spiritual enough to be clothed. Of course, the men and women in the Upper Room on the Day of Pentecost weren't that spiritual either. Peter, for example, had denied Jesus three times, but God uses imperfect vessels and clothes them with the Spirit to do His work.

When God clothes us in His Spirit, He actually clothes us with the joy of the Lord, because joy is wrapped up with the anointing.

The Joy of the Lord

In the Body of Christ today, we have seen an outpouring of the joy of the Lord, and it's such an important emotion, partly because it is wrapped up with the anointing. If you're experiencing the joy that the Lord gives, clearly you are clothing yourself in His Spirit, His anointing.

Now that we've made the assertion that joy is wrapped up with the anointing, let's prove it. Psalm 45:7 says, "God...hath anointed thee with the oil of gladness above thy fellows." This is a reference to Jesus, who is the head of the Body. So if the head is anointed with gladness, what will the Body be? Joyful.

But you may say, "Yes, but you don't know how bad my circumstances are." Then let's look at what the New Testament has to say about the joy of the Lord:

Looking unto Jesus the author and finisher of our faith; who for the joy that was set before him endured the cross, despising the shame, and is set down at the right hand of the throne of God.

Hebrews 12:2

How on earth did Jesus endure the anguish at the Garden of Gethsemane, the suffering of the Cross, taking the sin and sickness of the world upon Him, and bearing the rejection and cruelty of His own? He endured it for joy. He knew what joy lay before Him.

Once you've been baptized into the fullness of God's Spirit, you can walk in the same fullness of joy Jesus Himself walked in.

His joy was full once He was anointed. John the Baptist baptized Him, and the Spirit of the Lord came upon Him. (Luke 4:18.) From that time forward, Jesus began to walk and move in the fullness of the Spirit—and in the joy of the Lord.

Once you've been baptized into the fullness of God's Spirit, you can walk in the same fullness of joy Jesus Himself walked in. There's something about the baptism of the Holy Spirit that fills you with joy!

Joy comes with the anointing, and God is pouring out joy on people in these last days, because He's pouring out His anointing.

Isaiah 35:10 says, "And the ransomed of the Lord shall return, and come to Zion with songs and everlasting joy upon their heads." God wants to anoint you with joy. Enter into the joy of the Lord. Walk in it as you walk in the anointing of the Holy Spirit.

In fact, pray this with me right now: "Father, let the joy fall on my head today. I need Your joy. Let me enter into the joy and the strength You have for me. I receive it today. I'm not defeated; I'm a winner! And so I receive the beauty of Your joy in Jesus' name!"

Epilogue

My final prayer for you is that you enter into a new dimension of the Holy Spirit, a new power of the Holy Spirit, and a new relationship with God through the Holy Spirit. See Him as your Helper.

You're clothed in the anointing of the Holy Spirit, and that anointing resides in you as a temple—a temple housing the presence of God Himself.

I believe God has a wonderful plan for your life and a divine destiny for you. He knew you in the womb. He sent Jesus to die for you, and He's given you the Holy Spirit as a gift for the asking. As you enter into and operate in this gift, God will use you for His glory.

Epilogue

Endnotes

Chapter 1

[1] Webster, p. 1535, s.v. "comfort."

[2] Strong, "Greek," p. 55, entry #3875, s.v. "Comforter."

[3] Strong, "Greek," p. 55, entry #3844, s.v. "para."

[4] Strong, "Greek," p. 39, entry #2564, s.v. "kaleo."

Chapter 2

[1] Strong, "Greek," p. 59, entry #4152, s.v. "pneumatica."

[2] Strong, "Greek," p. 77, entry #5486, s.v. "charismata."

[3] Strong, "Greek," p. 22, entry #1248, s.v. "deacon."

Chapter 3

[1] Strong, "Hebrew," p. 10, entry #224, s.v. "urim," p. 125, entry #8550, s.v. "thummim."

[2] Strong, "Greek," p. 49, entry #3485, s.v. "naos."

[3] Strong, "Greek," p. 56, entry #4005, s.v. "Pentecost."

Chapter 4

[1] Strong, "Greek," p. 46, entry #3144, s.v. "witness."

[2] Strong, "Greek," p. 36, entry #2316, s.v. "Theos," p. 75, entry #5384, "phileo."

[3] Strong, "Greek," p. 24, entry #1411, s.v. "dunamis."

[4] Strong, "Greek," p. 61, entry #4342, s.v. "continued."

[5] Strong, "Greek," p. 8, entry #80, s.v. "brethren."

[6] Strong, "Greek," p. 46, entry #3167, s.v. "wonderful works."

7   Strong, "Greek," p. 42, entry #2842, s.v. "common."

8   Strong, "Greek," p. 27, entry #1618, s.v. "ektenes."

9   Strong, "Greek," p. 74, entry #5257, s.v. "minister."

10 Strong, "Greek," p. 27, entry #1681, s.v. "Elymas."

11 Strong, "Greek," p. 12, entry #450, s.v. "anistemi."

12 Strong, "Greek," p. 26, entry #1577, s.v. "ekklesia."

13 Strong, "Greek," p. 63, entry #4436, s.v. "divination."

14 Strong, "Greek," p. 66, entry #4691, s.v. "babbler."

15 Strong, "Greek," p. 21, entry #1140, s.v. "gods."

Chapter 5

1   Strong, "Greek," p. 28, entry #1746, s.v. "endued."

References

Conner, Kevin J., *Acts*. Portland: Bible Temple, 1973.

Dake, Finis Jennings, *Dake's Annotated Reference Bible*. Lawrenceville: Dake Bible Sales, Inc., 1963.

Lockyer, Herbert Sr., *Nelson's Illustrated Bible Dictionary*. Nashville: Thomas Nelson Publishers, 1986.

Phillips, John, *Exploring Acts,* vols. 1,2. Chicago: Moody Press, 1986.

Strong, James, *Strong's Exhaustive Concordance of the Bible,* "Hebrew and Chaldee Dictionary," "Greek Dictionary of the New Testament." Nashville: Abingdon, 1890.

Webster's New World Dictonary, Third College Edition. New York: Simon & Schuster, 1996.

Wilkinson, Bruce and Kenneth Boa, *Talk Thru the Bible*. Nashville: Thomas Nelson Publishers, 1983.

The Bethany Parallel Commentary on the New Testament. Minneapolis: Bethany House Publishers, 1983.

About the Author

Marilyn Hickey is no stranger to impacting the lives of millions worldwide. As founder and president of Marilyn Hickey Ministries, Marilyn is being used by God to help "cover the earth with the Word." Her mission has been effectively accomplished through various avenues of ministry, such as partnering with other ministries to ship thousands of Bibles into Communist countries; holding crusades in places like Ethiopia, the Philippines, Korea, Haiti, Brazil, Malaysia, Japan, and Honduras; and reaching individuals worldwide through television broadcasts seen on networks such as *Black Entertainment Network* (BET) and *Trinity Broadcasting Network* (TBN). In addition, Marilyn Hickey Ministries has established a fully accredited 2-year Bible college to raise up Christian leaders to carry out God's mission. Marilyn also serves the body of Christ as the Chairman of the Board of Regents for Oral Roberts University and is the only woman serving on the Board of Directors for Dr. David Yonggi Cho (pastor of the world's largest congregation, Yoido Full Gospel Church).

In addition to her ministry, Marilyn is also a busy wife and mother of two grown children. She is married to Wallace Hickey, pastor of Orchard Road Christian Center in Greenwood Village, Colorado.

Other Books by Marilyn Hickey

A Cry for Miracles

Angels All Around

Breaking Generational Curses

Devils, Demons and Deliverance

Godís Covenant for Your Family

How To Be a Mature Christian

Know Your Ministry

Maximize Your Day

Names of God

Release the Power of the Blood Covenant

Satan-Proof Your Home

Signs in the Heavens

When Only a Miracle Will Do

Your Total Health Handbook:
Spirit, Soul and Body

Beat Tension

Bold Men Win

Born-Again and Spirit-Filled

Bull Dog Faith

Change Your Life

Children Who Hit the Mark

Conquering Setbacks

Dare To Be An Achiever

Don't Park Here

Experience Long Life

Fasting and Prayer

God's Benefit: Healing

Hold on to Your Dream

How To Win Friends

Keys to Healing Rejection

More Than a Conqueror

Power of Forgiveness

Power of the Blood

Receiving Resurrection Power

Renew Your Mind

Seven Keys To Make You Rich

Solving Life's Problems

Speak the Word

Stand in the Gap

Story of Esther

Tithes, Offerings, Alms
God's Plan for Blessing You!

Winning Over Weight

Women of the Word

Receive Jesus Christ as Lord and Savior of Your Life.

The Bible says, "That if thou shalt confess with thy mouth the Lord Jesus, and shalt believe in thine heart that God hath raised him from the dead, thou shalt be saved. For with the heart man believeth unto righteousness; and with the mouth confession is made unto salvation" (Romans 10:9,10).

To receive Jesus Christ as Lord and Savior of your life, sincerely pray this prayer from your heart:

Dear Jesus,

I believe that You died for me and that You rose again on the third day. I confess to You that I am a sinner and that I need Your love and forgiveness. Come into my life, forgive my sins, and give me eternal life. I confess You now as my Lord. Thank You for my salvation!

Signed_____ Dated_____

Write to us.

We will send you information to help you
with your new life in Christ.

Marilyn Hickey Ministries • P.O. Box 17340
Denver, CO 80217 • (303) 770-0400

Or find us on the world-wide web:
www.mhmin.org

Prayer Requests

Let us join our faith with yours for your prayer needs.
Fill out below and send to:

Marilyn Hickey Ministries
P.O. Box 17340
Denver, CO 80217

Prayer Request_____

_____

_____

☐ Mr. & Mrs.   ☐ Mr.   ☐ Miss

Name _____

Address _____

City _____

State_____Zip _____

Home Phone (   )_____

Work Phone (   ) _____

Call for prayer TOLL-FREE, 24-hours a day 1-877-661-1249

Or leave your prayer request at our website/ministry center:
www.mhmin.org

WORD TO THE WORLD COLLEGE

Explore your options and increase your knowledge of the Word at this unique college of higher learning for men and women of faith. Word to the World College offers **on-campus and correspondence courses** that give you the opportunity to learn from Marilyn Hickey and other great Bible scholars, who can help prepare you to be an effective minister of the gospel. Classes are available for both full- and part-time students.

For more information, complete the coupon below and send to:

Word to the World College
P.O. Box 17340
Denver CO 80217
(303)770-0400

☐ Mr. & Mrs.   ☐ Mr.   ☐ Miss

Name _____

Address _____

City_____State_____Zip_____

Home Phone (   )_____

Work Phone (   ) _____

Or contact us on the world-wide web: www.mhmin.org

For Your Information
Free Monthly Magazine

Please send me your free monthly magazine OUTPOURING (including daily devotionals, timely articles, and ministry updates)!

Tapes and Books

Please send me Marilyn's latest product catalog.

☐ Mr. & Mrs.   ☐ Mr.   ☐ Miss

Name _____

Address _____

City _____

State_____Zip _____

Home Phone (   )_____

Work Phone (   ) _____

Mail to:

Marilyn Hickey Ministries
P.O. Box 17340
Denver, CO 80217
(303) 770-0400

TOUCHING YOU WITH THE LOVE OF JESUS!
Marilyn Hickey
PRAYER CENTER

When was the last time that you could say, "He touched me right where I hurt"? No matter how serious the nature of your call, we're here to pray the Word and show you how to touch Jesus for real answers to real problems.

Call us and let's touch Jesus, together!

Call for prayer TOLL-FREE, 24-hours a day:

1-877-661-1249

WE CARE!

Additional copies of this book
are available from your local bookstore.

HARRISON HOUSE
Tulsa, Oklahoma 74153

The Harrison House Vision

Proclaiming the truth and the power
Of the Gospel of Jesus Christ
With excellence;

Challenging Christians to
Live victoriously,
Grow spiritually,
Know God intimately.